God at the Mall

God at the Mall

Youth Ministry That Meets Kids Where They're At

PETE WARD

HENDRICKSON PUBLISHERS

Hendrickson Publishers, Inc.
P. O. Box 3473
Peabody, Massachusetts 01961–3473

Printed in the United States of America
ISBN 1–56563–411–X

First printing — September 1999

God at the Mall: Youth Ministry That Meets Kids Where They're At is revised and adapted from *Youthwork and the Mission of God: Frameworks for Relational Outreach,* and is published under agreement between Hendrickson Publishers, Inc., and the Society for Promoting Christian Knowledge.

First published in Great Britain 1997
Society for Promoting Christian Knowledge
Holy Trinity Church
Marylebone Road
London NW1 4DU

Library of Congress Cataloging-in-Publication Data

Ward, Pete, 1959–
    God at the mall: youth ministry that meets kids where they're at / Pete Ward; with a foreword by Dean Borgman.
    Includes bibliographical references.
    ISBN 1–56563–411–X (paper)
    1. Church work with youth.   I. Title.
BV4447.W36   1999
259'.23—dc21   99–33607
                                              CIP

To my friends in Young Life:

Arnie Jacobs, Les Comee,
Jack Carpenter, and Dean Borgman

Contents

Foreword

If there is one person who has stimulated me intellectually and professionally in regards to our mission of youth ministry, it is Pete Ward. He has encouraged my studies of culture, my writing, and my ties with other professionals around the world. Seven of his books are on my shelf.

So there may be some bias when I say Pete has had a profound impact on youth ministry in the United Kingdom and around the world as well. He has championed the idea of incarnational ministry—relational outreach to young people. His initiative brought together professors and trainers for bi-annual conferences in Oxford—and now an international association and a journal for our fledgling profession. Professors and leaders have all been very impressed with Pete's style and wisdom.

Pete Ward planned, and brought me in on, a dynamic presentation to the almost 2,000 Anglican bishops, spouses, and others meeting at their once-a-decade Lambeth Conference in the summer of 1998.

My professional relationship with Pete Ward goes back to the mid-1980s. Especially appreciative students have a tendency to stay in touch and leave messages like: "You ought to read . . ." or "You've got to meet . . ." So it was that Tina Freimuth, who was part of an Institute of Youth Ministries in

Colorado—and had gotten to meet and work with Pete Ward through Arnie Jacobs—told my wife Gail and me we *had* to stop off in England on the way back from an African trip and meet this Pete Ward. Ever since then Gail and I have enjoyed a special friendship with Pete, his wife Tess, and their two kids.

I have watched Pete grow a dynamic youth ministry, go on to develop that base into an exciting training program, begin to write challenging material on his experiences and the profession as a whole, become an advisor to the Archbishop and church at large, and then bring together professionals who had little contact with one another to theological reflection on cutting edge issues of our ministry.

Pete Ward is uniquely gifted as a cultural observer, as a musician, as one who can relate especially to rebellious young people, and as a leader of leaders as well as of youth.

Pete has always found holes in existing ministry and studies. He senses intellectual and ministerial vacuums, and wants to see them filled. Now, as a professor at King's College, London, his studies will continue to add to youthwork's professionalism. Many of Pete's missiological questions are just not being raised elsewhere. Christian Education circles have settled for issues that tend toward ingrown ministry. Education continues to be studied apart from striking cultural changes affecting the way young people grow, form their new adult identities, and develop communities. Paraparochial youth organizations tend to be disinterested in research and hard questions—they take note of current fads while resisting long-term evaluations of their ministries, which might correct possible errors or misplaced emphases. These are issues Pete continues to raise.

There is a critical need for sound research on youth and worship. This book raises issues about youth worship that beg further research. In it you will read about two separate disciplines of youth ministry and be challenged in regards to what is often left out of youth ministry. You will take a new look at relational youth ministry, be challenged to think about a deeper contextualization of the good news, and consider the relationship of youth and paraparochial organizations to the church. You will be encouraged to confront the growing phenomenon of youth churches. And you will certainly come back to the dynamic question: "How is new wine to be contained in old wineskins?"

A final word of caution: even in the UK Pete Ward is considered a bit provocative. As you read this you may feel a bit uncomfortable being confronted by this bright and challenging Brit. Please, push through it. Don't miss the crucial questions Pete is raising for our profession in these critical times.

Dean Borgman
Charles E. Culpeper Professor of Youth Ministries
Gordon-Conwell Theological Seminary
Director, Center for Youth Studies

Introduction

The story of this book is really the story of my own ministry with young people. In 1980 I was employed by St. Michael's Church, an Anglican church in Macclesfield, England. My job title was lay missionary and I was employed to work as an itinerant musician. This meant that I travelled around the country doing concerts and taking part in missions. Schools seemed to be the place for the aspiring Christian singer-songwriter at that time and I would often find myself alongside a Scripture Union worker presenting lessons and assemblies for unsuspecting pupils.

Three years of this work had left me with two convictions. The first was that I wanted to stop travelling around. The second was that there must be a better way of reaching out to young people than short-term missions. I solved the first problem by taking a job with St. Clement's Church in Oxford. Here my role was to run the church-based youth group and to play an active part in the life of the congregation (being active seemed to involve quite a lot of chair moving as far as I could see). My first idea in my new job was that I would try to take what I had learned from travelling around the country and apply it in my local situation. So along with other church youthworkers I set about running a school-based outreach in the Oxford area. The plan was that in each church there would be an evangelistic coffeehouse and these would be publicized through assemblies at lunch time events at the local school nearest to each of our churches. In this way we planned to run two or three coffeehouses in different parts of the city.

The plan was excellent and worked very well in the churches where there was a good-sized lively youth group. In the church I attended, however, we had only a very small group. This meant that we did not have the wide network of friendships between young people that was the basis for success in the other churches in town. Looking back, I am sure that a more experienced youthworker would have taken a lot more time to build up the existing group in the church, making sure that they were confident in themselves and their faith before setting out on a mission. My going the coffeehouse/school publicity route was a mistake, but I have to say that the experience of going to the local school during that mission changed my life.

I should explain that the person who has had the most influence over my work among young people is an American: Arnie Jacobs. I met Arnie for the first time when I started my job at St. Clement's. On my first day in the parish I found that Arnie had been booked to speak at the fellowship meeting. Of course, I had been around a bit, and I felt I knew it all and there was no way that an American, least of all one in his sixties, was ever going to teach me anything. As I listened, Arnie talked about the way that Jesus changed people's lives through relationships. He spoke about the need young people had for friendship with adults and how this could lead them to faith.

From my experience I knew that what Arnie was saying was true. I had seen young people changed while I had been visiting schools around the country. The problem was, I could recall occasions where my heart had ached as we drove away in the van and I could see no way that these young people would ever connect up with a local church. I had moved to Oxford precisely for this reason. Hit and run evangelism had left me searching for a better way.

Arnie worked for a US organization called Young Life, and he was generous enough to invite me to come and stay with him in Colorado Springs and find out more about what he called "incarnational evangelism." I was due to travel to Colorado the month after I finished my work in the schools, and I went knowing that I had given it my best shot in Oxford and it hadn't worked. Arnie took me to his local high school where I watched as he was greeted by groups of young people as we walked down the corridor. I was impressed with the warmth of relationship that he obviously had developed with them, and with their obvious delight in seeing him again. All this I found very challenging, but I wrote it off as an American thing. What did change my mind was the experience of meeting a small rock band at the school. They invited me back that evening to one of their rehearsals. Their openness was amazing, and as I confidently told Arnie that this sort of thing wouldn't happen in England, a group of boys at my local school came into my mind.

During my work in the schools near St. Clement's, at one of the lunch time concerts I had been surrounded by guys who wanted to talk with me. At the time I had found comments like, "My brother's got a guitar," and "I've got an amp," slightly amusing. In the light of my experience with Arnie I realized that these comments were an attempt on the part of these guys to build a relationship with me. They wanted friendship. Unfortunately I was so intent on my own agenda that I had missed what was an open invitation to get relational.

I came back from Colorado with several pairs of Levi's and a resolve to return to the school and try and meet these young people. I went to see the music teacher and arranged to offer informal guitar lessons at lunch times. Then I did another assembly and asked anyone who was in a band to meet me in the auditorium at break time. It was a success: I had a group of boys waiting to see me. Within a week or so I was meeting four or five groups of young people who were in bands, and there were about twenty beginners happily strumming away in the music room every Thursday lunch time. My ten years of relational youthwork at Oxford School had started. This work forms the backdrop to Chapter 3 of this book, where I explain relational youthwork as a theoretical model. Each stage in my journey is reflected in this chapter. The theory of relational outreach I present was generated by the questions raised by trying—not always with success—to find a way forward for the work with these young people.

In my first flush of enthusiasm I have to admit that I was much too critical of the fellowship group method of youthwork. I was convinced that the relational style of work was the only answer to the immense task of reaching out to the wide diversity of young people in British society. I realize now that my critical stance to what was the majority of church-based work was very unfair and somewhat misguided. In my defense I would say that I was filled with the enthusiasm of what I had found out. It has been my job with the Archbishop that has given me a much broader insight into the reality of youthwork on the street. Once again I am able to travel around the country, and my eyes have been opened. I have met so many church-based youth ministers who have seen remarkable success in their work that I have been forced to revise my opinions.

The result of this rethink is presented in Chapter 1, where I spell out what I call the two disciplines of youth ministry. I now understand the importance of both the relational and the fellowship group approaches to work with young people. In a way the seeds of this perspective were there in the first mission in the schools in Oxford, where the coffeehouses in the other churches were self-evidently successful. Further travels in the United States and contact with Young Life, however, has convinced me of the importance of relational "contact work" as an addition to the fellowship group style of ministry. How this could work is also spelled out in detail at the end of Chapter 1.

My journey of discovery in youth ministry has not been a solo effort. I have been extremely fortunate in working alongside a number of very skilled and insightful colleagues. The insights into relational youthwork presented in this book are very much a team effort. In 1988 Kenny Wilson from Scripture Union, Bob Dupee from Young Life in Canada, Tina Freimuth from Young Life U.S.A., and I started Oxford Youth Works. Oxford Youth Works was a course designed to train people in relational outreach. Over the years staff have come and gone, but each has contributed to our collective wisdom. I owe a good deal to these people; they are Jude Levermore, Sam Richards, Nick Allen, Anna Chakka George, Hannah Barnes, Lyn Wyatt, and Darren James.

As plans for the new training course were coming together, I felt the need to return to theological study. I spent two years travelling to Birmingham University where I did an M.A. in Religion and Culture. The course introduced me to two areas of thinking which have together enriched my understanding of youth ministry. The first is the sociology of youth subcultures. At Birmingham I became aware of the work of the Centre for Contemporary Cultural Studies. As a youthworker I was familiar with the richness of the cultural world of young people. Suddenly here was whole body of literature which was an aid to unlocking this world and developing ideas concerning the meaning of the way young people chose to act, dress, make music, etc. The subsequent result of my investigations into questions concerning youth culture and popular culture are presented in Chapter 4 of this book. The second area of thinking was the whole field of mission studies. While I was doing my M.A., I began to realize that the insights and approaches which were developing in countries around the world could be of considerable help in my own work with young people. While missionaries had started to develop theology in the culture and context of people in Africa, the Pacific Islands, Asia, and Latin America, it was clear to me that youth culture might be a context for similar exploration. Combining the insights from the study of youth cultures with the theological methods which were now commonplace in missiology might lead to a contextualized theology of young people. My current understanding of contextualization is presented in Chapter 5, and in Chapter 6 I develop these ideas in two short case studies to show how different styles of youth ministry might emerge from this kind of theological approach.

A contextualized theology of young people inevitably brings about changes in the church. My own journey in respect to the relationship between young people and the church has been affected by two very different experiences. The first came when I walked into the Big Top at Greenbelt, a Christian arts festival, and encountered the embryonic Nine O'Clock Service. The Nine O'Clock Service was the pioneer alternative worship service in England, using visuals and dance music. I stayed for only about ten minutes, but what I saw was enough of an inspiration to make me realize that contextualization of youth culture needed to be carried into the worship of the church. In Oxford I decided to work with the young people I knew to create a service which was based on their cultural expression. The result was a service we called JOY. Being creative in worship was a real challenge, and my reflections on this experience form the background to the second half of Chapter 7 on sacraments and creativity.

The second experience has come through my links with the Charismatic youth festival, Soul Survivor, where I have been very happy to form part of the team during the last three years. At Soul Survivor I have been exposed to the growing move toward the development of "Youth churches." I have had cause to revise my opinions once again, and these are the thoughts I present at the start of Chapter 7. Youth ministry is a growth area in the life of the church. The current scene is characterized by considerable innovation and experimentation. Amid all of this activity there is a need for some of us to take a few steps back from time to time and reflect on the way we are working with young people. This book represents my own thinking over the last few years. We all stand on the shoulders of those who went before us. I hope that others will read this and find it to be a helpful "leg up" in seeking to present Christ afresh in each generation.

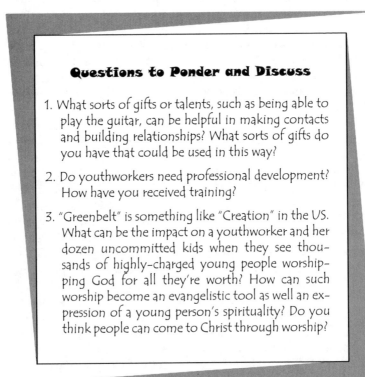

Questions to Ponder and Discuss

1. What sorts of gifts or talents, such as being able to play the guitar, can be helpful in making contacts and building relationships? What sorts of gifts do you have that could be used in this way?

2. Do youthworkers need professional development? How have you received training?

3. "Greenbelt" is something like "Creation" in the US. What can be the impact on a youthworker and her dozen uncommitted kids when they see thousands of highly-charged young people worshipping God for all they're worth? How can such worship become an evangelistic tool as well an expression of a young person's spirituality? Do you think people can come to Christ through worship?

The Two Disc/plines
of Youth Ministry:
Outside-In or Inside-Out?

hristian youthwork can be divided into two quite different traditions or disciplines.[1] The first tradition is characterized by work that starts with young people who have been brought up in the church, while the second has concentrated on ministry among those who are outside the church. From the pioneer days of youthwork in the 19th century these two basic approaches to Christian youthwork have been in evidence. Each generation of youthworkers has developed significant initiatives that broadly fall within these two areas. Some have focused their work on groups of Christian young people and others have concentrated on work with those who are outside the church. The methods of youthwork developed by Christians are divided by whether the work starts outside or inside the church. Similarly Christian youthwork organizations generally fall into one of these two traditions.

The first tradition can be called "Inside-Out" because it starts with young people who are inside the church. But one of the main aims of Christian groups formed from young people who are already believers is to attract new non-Christian members and introduce them to the faith. Thus Inside-Out starts with those inside who then reach out. The second tradition can be called "Outside-In," starting with those young people who are outside the church and working to bring them in eventually. These categories are in no way meant to imply that one tradition is primarily evangelistic and the other primarily concerned with nurturing already existing faith. Neither would it be correct to say that one is concerned solely with the church and the other with "society" at large. Rather the distinction made between these two traditions is based upon three main factors:

a) Where the work starts

b) The methodology adopted

c) Assumptions about culture and faith.

This chapter sets out the case for dividing youthwork into two traditions by exploring their distinctive starting points, methodologies, and assumptions. The differences between these two kinds of youthwork are then explored in greater detail. Before that, however, there are some introductory remarks that need to be made concerning the use of the terms "youthwork" and "youth ministry" and also the understanding of "traditions" and "discipline" which shape the structure of this book.

Youthwork and Youth Ministry◆◆◆◆◆◆◆◆◆◆◆◆◆◆

We are currently experiencing a resurgence of Christian work among young people. These are very exciting times to be involved in Christian youthwork. New initiatives and projects are springing up all around the country. Since the early 1980s more and more youthworkers are being employed by churches and Christian organizations. One result of this has been that we are seeing increasing experimentation in the way that Christians work with young people.

The use of the term "youth ministry" is linked to this new wave of full-timers. Many of us felt that our methods of working gave us a distinctive identity. In particular we were aware that professional "youthworkers" were those who had passed through recognized "secular" youth and community courses. The new developments in Christian work among young people, however, were not connected with "youthwork" in the secular professional sense, being more firmly rooted in Christian perspectives and in many cases directly funded by the church. The term youth ministry reflects the feeling that much of what passes for "youthwork" in a secular setting is of a different genus than the new kinds of work being funded by the church.

"Youth ministry" in this sense is an attempt to express that there is an approach to youthwork which operates within a code different from that developed within "secular youthwork" but which is also professional. This method of work should be called "ministry" because its closest partner remains the clergy who also refer to their practice as "ministry." Some have expressed this relationship more explicitly by adopting the title "Youth Pastor." It would be possible to speak of those who work Inside-Out as youth ministers and those who work Outside-In as Christian youthworkers. Alongside these patterns of work there may also be Christians who work within projects which follow the "secular" philosophy generally associated with "youth and community work."

These distinctions, while containing some sense of these two terms, remain a little unsatisfactory. In the first instance, "youthwork" has never been solely applied to work in secular settings. Christians have also used the term for both work within the church and work outside. For Christians, youthwork has historically been a broad term covering evangelism and Christian nurture as well as the principles and values advocated by youth and community work courses. A Christian youthworker therefore might be engaged in either of these areas. In terms of the two traditions discussed in this book, therefore, it would be misleading to speak of the church-based work as youth ministry and work outside the church as "youthwork."

A further factor in the use of these terms is that many Christians feel that their work, while "outside the church," has a deep spiritual significance. The ministry of the church is seen as being to both those inside and those outside the church. Youth ministry therefore is a term that could express this fact. It is also the case that many Christians who have been trained in "secular" youthwork courses and are employed in the public sector see part of their work with young people in spiritual terms. The present widespread interest in spiritual development for youth signals that the labelling of the statutory sector as "secular" is somewhat of a misnomer.[2] There are indications in the areas of practice and of training that Christian perspectives may well find an increasing acceptance by the wider youthwork community.[3]

The confusion over terminology is a result of new developments in Christian work among young people. Those who wish to locate themselves firmly within the church may well choose "youth ministry," while those working in regular contact with government-sponsored work among youth may well prefer "youthwork." My own feeling is that the use of the term youth ministry solely for work inside the church and youthwork for work outside the church tends to perpetuate a sacred/secular divide which I would not wish to support. My experience with working with groups from the church and with young people from outside a Christian context is that my role is to be a kind of amphibian able to exist in the water and on the land. Youthworker as frog may not be an attractive proposition, I realize, but the ability to change environments comfortably is a basic skill required of all youthworkers. The youthworker who is locked in a church context is evangelistically and culturally severely limited. The youthworker able to relate only to non-Christians doesn't get a job (or if he or she gets it, conflict with the church soon ensues). It is the ability to move successfully between the world of the Christian church and the world of young people which characterizes successful youthwork of either tradition.

For these reasons I have decided to use "youthwork" and "youth ministry" interchangeably in this book.

Tradition and Discipline◆◆◆◆◆◆◆◆◆◆◆◆◆◆◆◆◆◆◆◆

Christian youthwork has survived by the ability to develop patterns of work and shared values. In most cases these patterns have been handed down from individual to individual within the structures provided by voluntary organizations.

Tradition in this sense is well understood by those within organizations such as Youth for Christ, Young Life, Campus Crusade, or Inter-Varsity Christian Fellowship.[4] Tradition, however, can also be used to describe the similarities which exist across organizational boundaries. The analysis of Christian youthwork in this chapter is based on dividing the majority of work into two different groups. These are hypothetical models created to give a broad understanding of what is a fairly diverse scene. Sociologists would speak of these models as ideal types. An ideal type is a theoretical construct or generalization. The generalization is used to make a clear picture from a number of complicated and seemingly different situations. An ideal type summarizes in a simplified form the basic characteristics of a way of working or behaving.[5] Each of the "traditions" of Christian youthwork, Outside-In and Inside-Out, is therefore an ideal type. The generalization attempts to describe how a number of separate and varied youthwork practices developed by Christians in different places and in different times might be categorized and therefore more clearly understood.

The use of generalizations or "ideal types" has a number of drawbacks. In the first instance the way we do youth ministry is extremely diverse, and the distinctions which we understand between one way of working and another can be very subtle. To generalize about only two basic traditions may therefore be seen as reductive and inaccurate. Individual youthworkers may feel that their work moves between and beyond the descriptions offered. This may well be the case, and I recognize that this sensitivity has some validity. Ideal types are not, however, designed to be a complete description of everything that is happening in youth ministry. The idea of two traditions is a useful tool because it offers a clarity of thought in what can at times be a fairly complex and confusing situation. The validity of the insights offered, by what I freely admit is a theoretical construct, depends upon the extent to which it sheds light on our practice as Christian youthworkers.

Linked to the idea of tradition is that of "discipline." It is understood that public high school teachers operate within a quite different discipline from that of youthworkers. Teaching is a separate profession from youthwork and it therefore operates within a quite different discipline. This means that it is possible to work with the same group of young people both as youthworker and as a teacher, but to do so successfully involves the ability to switch between the two disciplines. If a teacher working in a youth club fails to change the style of relating to young people and tries to act as a teacher in this new setting, then problems begin to emerge. Young people become unresponsive, or even resentful of what they feel is an inappropriate discipline (I mean this in both senses of the word). For the youthworker who enters a classroom setting but who fails to adopt the discipline of teaching, different problems come to the surface. Young people in my experience tend to riot! Teachers often acknowledge that youthwork represents a different approach to working with young people by saying that they would not want to try to be a youthworker with young people they also teach. In other words, while they might be able to switch disciplines, such a move is more problematic when dealing with the same young people. The reason these problems arise is that teaching and youthwork are two quite different disciplines.

The recognition that teaching and youthwork represent distinctive and separate ways of working with young people is widespread. Indeed while it was once the case that trained teachers were also seen as being qualified as social workers for youth, this is no longer the case in England. It is my argument that a similar kind of distinction needs to be brought into play between those youthworkers who work from inside the church out to the unchurched and those who start by ministering solely among the unchurched and hope to see them embrace the faith. Whether such a distinction should also be institutionalized in training for youth ministry I am as yet undecided. The main purpose at this stage of arguing for such a division is to gain clarity within the present youthwork scene.

The discipline of youth ministry expressed as a set of rules can be seen in a set of commonly experienced and understood social relationships. The ways youthworkers and young people relate to each other and behave within a practical youthwork setting is linked to these rules. The problems which youthworkers experience on a regular basis can be explained by a lack of clarity concerning the nature of the two disciplines. An example of this would be the trouble youthworkers experience when they try to connect a group of unchurched young people to a church group or when young people from outside the church behave inappropriately in a church service. Both of these situations can be much better understood and appropriate action taken if it is realized that work with Christian groups and work with un-churched groups are very different. The problem has come about because of a lack of clarity or because of a desire to blur the distinction between the two approaches. Youth ministry works best when we are clear in our own minds which discipline we are working within. One reason for this is that each discipline has its own internal logic. This not only dictates the structure of the work; it also applies to the way relationships are built and developed. The disciplines have slightly different approaches to working with both groups and individuals. Each discipline has different ways in which the Christian message is proclaimed, young people are nurtured in the faith, and they then relate to the local church.

Clarity concerning the particular discipline which is in operation is essential for successful work to grow and develop. At its most basic level there needs to be a consistency in youthwork practice so that the young people involved know where they are. For the youth minister there needs to be a clarity in order that the structure and strategy of a particular project might evolve successfully. For churches or youthwork agencies there needs to be an understanding developed with the worker(s) so that expectations are realistic and accountability can be maintained. It is my belief that many of the problems experienced by young people, youth ministers, and those managing youthwork projects stem from a lack of clear thinking about the tradition of youthwork and the appropriate discipline which is required for this tradition to work well.

First Discipline: Nucleus-Fringe Outreach (Inside-Out) ♦♦♦♦♦♦♦♦♦♦♦♦♦♦♦♦♦♦♦♦♦♦♦♦♦♦♦♦

Inside-Out youthwork starts by gathering together a group of young people who are already connected to the life of the church. Often the children of Christian parents are invited to form the basis of the group.[6] Sometimes the group will have graduated from the Sunday school classes in the church or from a confirmation group. The group may well have a title such as the "Youth Group" or "Youth Fellowship." Through a combination of social activities and a program of teaching, prayer, and worship, the group is encouraged and built up in the faith. In this way they form a "nucleus" of lively Christians. The core group, however, are also encouraged to invite other young people to join the group. Evangelism is a major priority in the group's life together.

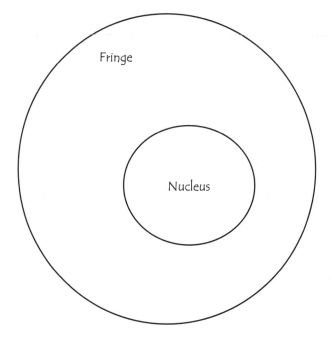

Outreach, therefore, happens most effectively when these young people are in ongoing relationships with non-Christians at school or in other social activities. The network of social contact which these young people sustain is vital to the evangelistic capabilities of the youthwork. The friends of group members can be seen as another group spread around the nucleus, often referred to as the fringe of the group. A fringe member might also be someone with church connections who attends occasionally. The social activities of the group may well be organized to facilitate the natural process whereby fringe members might become part of the group.

Those who work within this tradition of youth ministry emphasize that young people are by definition in touch with youth culture. As Tricia Williams puts it, "Teenagers may not have the maturity or depth of teaching of older Christians, but they are still the ones who are best equipped to communicate with their peers at school. They speak the language, they understand the trends in fashion and music; they share the same concerns and interests."[7] The feeling that young people are fully involved in the teenage world has led some people to suggest, "The best people to reach out to young people are young people themselves."[8]

The vast majority of Christian youthwork adopts a nucleus-fringe or Inside-Out approach. Most church youth groups operate within this tradition. Most Christian outreach relies upon the basic dynamic of a Christian young person inviting someone they already know along to a meeting or an event. The pattern for town, school, and university missions bears this out. Success of a mission does not really depend on the abilities of the evangelist or the team of helpers. Success invariably depends upon the active participation of young people. If they do not invite fringe people, one of two things happens: either the mission goes ahead with only Christians attending or it attracts large numbers of unchurched young people but they generally do not stay with the faith because they are not relationally linked to any of the church-based groups.

Friendship between Christian young people and non-Christians forms the basis for the majority of Christian youthwork, including most in-school outreach, Alpha Groups, Christian concerts, coffeehouses, and alternative worship services. Some of the more recent initiatives involving worship or outreach in night clubs may well attract large numbers of unchurched young people, but long term evangelistic success will almost certainly rely upon a committed group of Christian young people inviting unchurched young people to get more involved in the activities of their group. Having said this, adult youth ministers and volunteer youthworkers remain key in any nucleus-based work, although their role tends to be one of support, encouragement, and backup to the friendship outreach of the group members.[9] Adults may well see their role as running a program which provides the context within which young people can invite their friends to meet their Savior. In addition adults will work to build relationships with new members, but this will generally be within the context of the regular activities of the group.

The Limitations of the Nucleus-Fringe Approach ♦♦♦♦♦♦♦♦♦♦♦♦♦♦♦♦♦♦♦♦♦♦♦♦♦♦♦♦♦♦♦♦♦

The strengths of this tradition of Christian youthwork are unfortunately also its weaknesses. Christian young people are indeed connected through common educational and social activities with a potential fringe group, so friendship between young people provides the potential for sharing the gospel and attracting new members into the center of the group's activity. Involvement with the youth group leads non-Christians gently into an encounter with Christ in a supportive environment. The problem is that the social connections of young people are nearly always limited. Most of us make friends with people who are socially very similar to ourselves. Like almost always attracts like. The nucleus-fringe tradition of youthwork is therefore limited by its starting point. If the group is formed around one type of young person, then the likelihood is that it will attract only similar young people.[10] A predominance of relatively wealthy middle class young people in our group will lead to a middle class group. The young people coming to faith will be "unchurched," but they will be the "unchurched" of a particular type. Reliance on friendship evangelism ensures that we reach only those young people who fit the existing social make-up of the group.

Joining a church group may be attractive for some young people because it offers a route to move up the social scale. There will be some young people who do not precisely fit the social mix. Those who are socially fairly distant from the regular make-up of the church tend to join in ones and twos. In later life these young people are sometimes seen as trophies by a slightly patronizing church leadership. "That's Jim, he grew up on welfare in the projects," we hear the minister boast. Unfortunately, for every young person that does join the church there are probably ten or twenty other young people who have tried to find a place within the church but who found the social make-up of the congregation too uncomfortable. They feel that they do not fit and so conclude that the Christian faith is not for people like them.

The nucleus-fringe approach is favored by Christian youthworkers because it is extremely successful in socializing young people into the life of the church. As new members join the group they are also introduced to the behaviors, beliefs, values, and language of the wider church community. In most cases church attendance is actively encouraged. The close relationship between the church and the nucleus approach is both a strength and a weakness.

The nucleus approach is therefore limited by the extent to which the local church is able to accommodate a variety of social groups within its life and worship. While a youthworker may be able to develop contact with a group of local young people who are from the neighborhood of the church, it is very often the case that these young people find it hard to gain acceptance by the existing church membership. In some cases disapproval of the dress and behavior of young people may be overtly expressed by church members or by clergy.[11] If this is not the case then the language and assumptions of education and literacy which generally characterize worship simply serve to alienate the young people. In some cases they express this by disruptive behavior, but more often they simply conclude that church is not for them.

Second Discipline: Incarnational Outreach (Outside-In) ◆◆◆◆◆◆◆◆◆◆◆◆◆◆◆◆◆◆◆◆◆◆◆◆◆◆◆◆◆◆

From the earliest days Christians working with young people have recognized that they need to develop two different strategies. The first works with young people committed to the church and subsequently attracts people in. The second is primarily aimed at those who are socially distant from the church.

In the 19th century Christians talked about work that seeks out the "poor" or the "ragged." In more recent times we have recognized that there are particular needs among those fringe young people.

In every generation some Christian youthworkers have felt called to develop initiatives which are aimed at those communities and groups perceived, for whatever reason, to be distant from the make-up of the church. Organizations such as the YMCA bear witness to this calling. These organizations are part of the youthwork heritage of the Christian community, but they do not represent what we should see as the mainstream of Christian work among young people. The present day Christian youthwork scene is characterized by the nucleus-fringe tradition of work, and when churches talk about youthwork they almost always are talking about this tradition. The reason for this, as far as I see, is not a lack of social concern. As I have said, each generation during the last 150 years has sought to share the gospel with those seen as falling outside the predominantly middle class nature of the church. The problem has been that in most cases these particular initiatives have seen only partial success.[12] Working Outside-In is very challenging and is prone to failure. In contrast the nucleus-fringe approach goes from strength to strength when it typically targets privileged social groups. While the nucleus-fringe approach may well be the main approach adopted by Christians it is important to recognize that Christians working Outside-In have been the pioneers who have in many cases developed approaches and methods of working that have been taken up by the wider youthwork world. Work that is funded by government agencies is often based upon values and methods of work that were originally pioneered by the church seeking to share the Christian faith and show social concern with those outside the church. Over the last forty years this work has been secularized by the non-church youthwork profession.[13]

To work Outside-In is to step outside predominantly Christian groups. It is to move youthwork beyond a church setting into the local community. Outside-In means that youthworkers aim to work with individuals, groups, or communities who are socially and culturally distant from the existing church. The youthworker moves outside the Christian group to "be with" those who are outside the life of the church. "Being with" is adopted as a means of sharing the gospel. It is for this reason that many people who have explored this tradition have seen their work are being "incarnational" in nature. By using the term "incarnational" in this way, I do not mean to imply that only those who work Outside-In are following the example of Jesus. The ministry of adults and young people in a nucleus group is equally an imitation of Christ. I use the term therefore in a technical way as it is commonly used in missiology to denote the crossing of barriers to share the faith by being with a group of people.

The incarnation of Jesus is interpreted as an example of the way that those working Outside-In should minister. In the life of Jesus we see God becoming a human being to build relationship with humanity. In the same way the youthworker goes to a particular group of young people to share the gospel. While the nucleus group is based upon unchurched young people joining in with the activities of the group, working Outside-In requires the youthworker to participate in the life of unchurched young people. The nucleus tradition invites people in, the incarnational tradition goes out with the aim that young people may eventually join in the life of the church.

"Being with" gives the relational basis from which evangelism might develop. Those working Outside-In often speak of "meeting young people where they are at." This often involves focusing upon particular needs, thus the emphasis of the work may well include attention to issues such as drugs, homelessness, teenage pregnancy, and alcohol. It might be that in a particular town or area young people are seen as a "problem" by members of the church or by the wider community. Working Outside-In may well come about because of the needs of adults to feel that something is being done for or about "the kids."

A common response of the church to the challenge of working Outside-In has been to develop informal halfway houses where young people and youthworkers are able to meet. The open youth club has been the primary example of this. In the open club young people are invited to take part in activities or just to sit around. Workers will seek to build relationships with them in the context of the activities.[14] A similar plan can be seen in groups which run a Drop in Center or Alcohol Free

Bar or Advice Center. In all of these the young people remain within their own friendship groups. They are not expected to abandon their shared behaviors or values. The youth minister is seeking to meet them on their own turf. Of course the need to maintain rules and basic standards of behavior within a club or other activity will mean that the youth minister will have to come to some agreement with the groups of young people attending.

Alongside the provision of places where encounters between youthworkers and young people can take place, this tradition of youthwork has tended in more recent times to move toward a more detached approach. In detached youth ministry a youthworker or workers will attempt to build contact with young people on the streets, in a school, or wherever groups gather together. Detached work in some Christian circles has been referred to as relational youthwork with its emphasis upon relationships rather than on programs or the provision of open clubs in buildings.

The Limitations of the Incarnational Approach♦♦

Working Outside-In is extremely demanding and difficult. To journey outside the boundaries of the Christian community to share the gospel is a tough assignment. While youthwork within the church offers a safe and well-defined context for ministry, this may well not be the case for those working Outside-In. Workers need to be those able to combine a pioneer spirit with a commitment to remain faithful to a Christian perspective. Such youthwork not only means that Christians need to go though special training, it also requires the right kind of people. To be involved and perhaps more importantly to remain involved over the long haul is essential. This is a matter of discernment and balance. Journeying "outside" in order that young people might eventually find a place "inside" not only asks a good deal of the youth minister, it also requires understanding and flexibility from those churches and Christians who support the work.

There is no doubt that young people can be very needy. Working Outside-In will often involve a particular focus on young people who are in crisis or facing particular challenges. Tough problems are rarely solved overnight. Needy young people need adults who are able to offer long-term care and support. All of these issues mean that the church may well not be able to work Incarnationally/Outside-In without employing the right kind of people with the right kind of skills and training.

The particular challenges which face any youth minister working Outside-In mean that effective evangelism may well be a bridge too far. Faced with the considerable problems, first of building a trusting relationship with young people outside the church and second of the challenge of the particular crises or issues with which these young people are wrestling, the worker may well feel swamped. The pain and suffering of young people can leave a youthworker feeling at a loss as to how Christ might become real in their lives.[15] This might be because problems such as homelessness or drug abuse make the direct preaching of the gospel feel inappropriate. Young people need to be free to choose Christ for themselves, not be manipulated or coerced into commitment when they are off balance and vulnerable. Evangelism among young people who are culturally outside the church must be contextual as well as sensitive. Many youthworkers find the challenge of expressing the faith in relevant ways to be extremely demanding. There is a tendency for proclamation of the gospel to be downplayed or ignored entirely because it is seen as being so difficult to do well. A further factor may be that Christian groups seeking money from government agencies may experience pressure to adopt a less evangelistic style of work in order to receive funding. In addition to this there is the realization that even when young people do come to faith it is felt to be very unlikely that they will be welcomed into the life of the church.

The Dynamics of the Traditions ♦♦♦♦♦♦♦♦♦♦♦♦

The distinction drawn between working Inside-Out and working Outside-In is primarily based upon the starting point of each of the traditions. The argument that these are in fact two different disciplines is justified by a consideration of the internal dynamics of each of the approaches. These dynamics create fundamental differences in the two approaches. They are extremely powerful in the way that the different kinds of youthwork are operated and develop, and they mean that the two approaches are distinct.

♦The Community Context

The nucleus approach is intimately connected to the need for Christian parents to feel that their young people are "safe." In "Growing Up Evangelical" I have argued at some length that the function of evangelical youthwork is to provide a safe place where Christian young people can socialize.[16] This relationship between the youthwork and the needs and desires of Christian parents forms a strong undercurrent to all of the activities, values, and Christian teaching delivered within a church-related group. In all negotiations with the clergy or with a local church, the youthworker is working within the basic emotional dynamic which is created by the parental duties, needs, and concerns of church members. This dynamic is extremely powerful, and its influence cannot be underestimated. How evangelism takes place, how young people are nurtured within the faith, and how the group relates to church, will be determined by consultation among the clergy, the youthworker, young people, and Christian parents. In the majority of cases the parents supported by the clergy will form the most influential lobby pressuring the youthworker and the young people. This pressure is commonly felt when working Inside-Out.

When we move into the wider community and work Outside-In we find that not only the method of working has to change. More importantly the pressure which comes from the quite justified concerns of Christian parents does not form any part of the atmosphere within which the work progresses. Clergy and parents are not on the sidelines approving or disapproving of what is going on. The youth minister is therefore not subject to influence and lobbying which can very often form part of the church scene. When we work incarnationally among a group of young people the key dynamic which operates will be the relationship between the gospel commitments of the worker and the already existing values of the local community. Parents of young people and the wider community will judge the appropriateness of the work according to their own moral framework. The task of the youth minister is to work contextually, to start by respecting the already existing morality and values of the community within which they are working. In any community there will be ways of behaving and relating which not only are seen as "right" but might also be regarded by the Christian as a vestige or reflection of the kingdom of God. To work Outside-In is to start by affirming the positive in a particular community. To fail to do so will mean that the wider community of parents and neighbors and community leaders will see the work as a disruptive intrusion.

◆Assuming a Subculture

The nucleus approach assumes the subculture of the church to be the appropriate medium for evangelism and Christian worship. To join a nucleus group is to participate in a process of socialization into an already existing church subculture. This subculture is characterized by a common set of behaviors, language, values, and perspectives. Within the subculture of the church it may well be the case that the youth ministry will be innovative or even seen as on the edge in one way or another. This does not, however, mean that the youth ministry has moved from one subculture to another. In most cases youth ministry which is pioneering will be the means by which the church subculture renews itself. Church young people grow up to become key members of local churches. The youth leaders of today will often be the church leaders of tomorrow. These leaders take with them the insights and methods of working which they adopted in their youth ministry. In this way the youth ministry of fifteen years ago became the mainstream of church life today. One of the places where this is most obvious is the change in music used in church services. Most evangelical churches now have some kind of guitar-based music group leading worship. This practice has its roots in the youthwork of the 1960s and 1970s.

The nucleus discipline therefore works within an already contextualized expression of the faith. The church subculture is a cultural construction which connects the values of the gospel with a particular social context. To argue that church subculture is one possible expression of the Christian faith in our context is not the same as saying that this subculture is "wrong." It is simply to say that outside the subcultural context of the church this expression of the faith needs to be re-evaluated. Working incarnationally as opposed to the nucleus approach does not assume the subculture of the church to be normative. To work Outside-In is to seek to see the gospel contextualized among a group of people who were not previously part of the church. The hope is that Jesus can become real within the subculture which these people share. To say this is not to baptize a particular subculture uncritically. The gospel will act redemptively to bring about the values and behaviors which are characteristic of the kingdom of God. Redemption will involve an affirmation of some aspects of subcultural life and a critique of others. The priority will however be that the youth ministry will not seek to impose an expression of the faith which has evolved in one particular social context. The aim throughout will be to see people begin to live out the Christian faith with integrity and faithfulness within their own community context.

For the youthworker this process involves a journey of discovery. In the first place there is a need to set aside the security which the certainties of church work offer. Within a missiological context Charles Kraft has used the language of paradigm shift to describe the movement of the gospel and of the missionary from one cultural context to another.[17] This shift does not deny the validity of what a church context has taught us, it just recognizes that true engagement with different cultures and subcultures raises different questions of the Christian faith and of the Bible. From these questions emerges an interpretation of the faith which should remain true to the gospel and yet nuanced in a way which is fresh and distinctive.

◆The Rules of the Discipline

The nucleus approach operates within a set of clearly defined rules. How young people are expected to behave in their

24

personal lives and in the life of the group is closely defined. Issues to do with sex, drugs, alcohol, swearing, smoking, etc. will be discussed frequently, and expectations will be made very clear. When the rules of the group are breached in some way, the leaders will take steps to try to normalize the situation.

The strict adherence to behavioral codes arises from the well-defined standards expected by Christian parents and the church. When youthworkers allow groups to step beyond these rules, serious problems start to emerge. If, for instance, a youth group is found to be involved with drugs, the youthworker may be relieved of his or her position. Christian young people and parents expect, and most probably need, a fairly well-defined setting within which to explore the Christian faith. When youthworkers allow a freer interpretation of the rules, it is not unusual for Christian young people go a little over the top. The youth group party where young people get drunk would be a good example of this kind of problem. Clear boundaries and rules are essential to the successful working of a nucleus group. They form a part of the package, and while they may be renegotiated a little, they are properly part of the scenery. In contrast, when youthworkers work Outside-In, a much more complicated picture begins to emerge.

To work incarnationally is to start by accepting young people as they are. The worker is first wanting to build a non-judgmental relationship which means understanding before setting down rules. This means that a worker may well be witness to and aware of behavior that is not only inappropriate for the church youth group but also may be illegal. The worker may well conclude that some of what passes for normal behavior in the group (e.g., racist comments) is completely out of step with the gospel. How this perspective may be shared involves a negotiation between worker and young people. The worker will need to make a decision as to the extent to which such things will be allowed to pass because the worker wishes to remain in relationship with the group or individual. Alongside this the workers will need to balance the extent to which their presence, or their silence, compromises their integrity as Christian youth ministers. Such a dilemma does not occur in working in a nucleus group—or at least it should not!—while it is the everyday stuff of working Outside-In.

The manner of the youth minister who engages with a group incarnationally will need to be primarily that of a learner. While the behavior of the group may well clash with the values of the worker at first, the aim is to move beyond this to find the underlying values of the group. The good which is there in every subculture could take a little time to become evident, and the worker needs to gain understanding. It is only out of a sympathetic knowledge of both the good and the bad that the worker can present Jesus as someone who can meet the group within their own cultural world. The aim is that behavior and values emerge from a transformational encounter between Jesus and the group. The hope is that as this begins to come about, the group become distinctively followers of Jesus within their own subcultural context. To help this to come about, the worker needs to be able to change from someone who is building relationships and understanding to someone who is a leader within that group context. The ability to effect this change in role, from observer to one who is seeking to bring about change and renewal, is fundamental to success in incarnational ministry. This aspect of working incarnationally is qualitatively different from the discipline of work in a church context.

◆Church

The nucleus group is generally rooted in a church setting. The young people who make up the core of the group will often come from church-going committed families. Most groups are formally linked to one particular church. While the church may well see the need for separate activities, and even different worship services, for the young people, the links will, in most cases, remain strong. The young people of the church are rightly seen as a vital part of the whole community of the church body. Theologically and practically this means that young people in a nucleus group really cannot be talked about as if they are a separate church. They form a part of the wider Christian community however their meetings are organized. Having said this, the reality is that young people meeting together are part of the church. When young people from church families and their friends start to experiment with worship, it is important that ways are found to express the genuine "churchness" of what they are doing.[18]

When working Outside-In, the relationship between this new group of Christian young people and the church is a little less clear. To see the gospel contextualized in a cultural setting that is distinct from the existing local church may well mean that what is appropriate would be something more akin to the planting of a new church. The eventual aim of the work would be the establishment of a new church which reaches out to people of all ages within that particular subculture. This new church will need to come to some resolution with the wider church community. My own feeling is that such initiatives need the tradition, stability, and support of existing denominations or church groups to avoid going down the route of a narrow and authoritarian sectarianism. To church plant in this manner involves very different skills and structures from work in a nucleus/church setting.

Mixing Up the Disciplines ◆◆◆◆◆◆◆◆◆◆◆◆◆◆◆◆◆

The argument for dividing Christian youthwork into two separate but complementary disciplines is primarily based on the need for clarity. It is fundamental to my argument that both of these traditions of youthwork have a place in the life of the church. The nucleus model has come about because the church has duty to bring up its own young people in the faith. This approach is rightly evangelistic. Indeed Bob Clucas argues that without the steady involvement of non-Christian young people in youth groups and Christian Camps and House parties, the nucleus model simply doesn't work. Clucas argues, and I think rightly, that Christian young people need to feel that the faith has the power to change people.[19] They are themselves therefore built up in the faith by seeing their friends come to faith. A nucleus group which does not have a regular injection of new enthusiasm and members tends to stagnate.

The church, however, also has a duty to share the gospel message with the wider community. But while every church should seek to encourage its own teenagers to remain a part of the church, it is probably not the case that every church should engage in working Outside-In. This is partly a matter of resources. To engage incarnationally with communities distant from the church is costly and involves particular skills and resources. It is therefore probably more realistic to expect groups of churches in an area to supplement the nucleus model by joining together to support a more experimental model of incarnational outreach. In some cases this is best done through setting up an independent charitable group dedicated to this kind of work or by forming a partnership with an existing para-church group such as Youth For Christ or Young Life. Churches will always be inclined to look to helping their own young people before they engage in mission among other groups. This I feel is very proper. However, there probably needs to be a decision to tithe to support Outside-In work. One approach might be for churches in an area who are appointing youthworkers to join together and agree that at least one of the posts should focus upon groups of young people who are unlikely to be touched by the nucleus approach.

Work that is Outside-In is vulnerable to subversion by the church. Most churches are committed to outreach, but they habitually see this in terms of the Inside-Out model of ministry. When Outside-In work begins to get going, the habitual values and behaviors of the church seem to gently take the power and energy out of the ministry. This will never be a deliberate policy. It simply emerges when the two disciplines are confused or when attempts are made to merge the two approaches, for instance, when involvement in the existing youth group or church is seen as the next step for young people who have come to faith through incarnational outreach in the local community. While occasionally this strategy may work, more often than not enthusiastic and articulate local young people have the energy sapped from them because they are introduced to the more developed and authoritative subculture of the church group. Suddenly the lively and original ways in which they first spoke of their new Christian experience are replaced by the standardized jargon of the church. In some cases these new young people simply fade from the Christian scene. If they remain involved with the church they tend to become disconnected from their home culture and communities by the socializing nature of the

Christian group. In the church group they become more Christian but they can also become more middle class.

The subversion of Outside-In work can also come about when youthworkers themselves blur the boundaries. One example of this I have heard of involved a group of unchurched young people who came to faith through outreach on the streets. The worker realized that a separate worship service which emerged from their culture would probably be the best next step. Soon a lively worship service got underway using dance music and visuals as well as a commitment to charismatic ministry. Local church groups soon got to hear of this event, and they started to come along. Soon an event which was based on 50 or so unchurched young people had grown to become a mixed group of 400 churched and unchurched. The success of the service was amazing and the worker and his team were very excited. The problem was that within a year every one of the unchurched young people had disappeared from the service. None of them made a fuss; they seemed to go very quietly. In fact they went so quietly that the youthworker didn't even notice. The departure of the original group was disguised by the roller coaster success of the service.

Blurring the boundaries often comes about when churches are appointing full-time youthworkers. The job descriptions of church youthworkers are a horror genre all of their own. Chief among these horrors, in my view, is the inability of committees and clergy to resolve the problem of which type of youth ministry they expect to see happening in their church. An idealism sets in which then means that both approaches are expected of the same person. Most of us have a commitment both to work with young people in the church and to outreach to those who will not join our church groups. Unfortunately, in my experience, very few of us are able to sustain active and lively ministry in both of these areas at the same time. The reality is that we favor either one or the other. Over time problems begin. If we favor Outside-In over Inside-Out work, we may end up losing our jobs because Christian parents and clergy perceive us as failing. If we favor Inside-Out work over Outside-In, then we may keep the church happy but we may not achieve all we hope for in our outreach work.

At heart these problems arise from a misunderstanding of the importance of both of the disciplines of youth ministry.

In many people's minds evangelism to the unchurched inevitably means some kind of Outside-In model of ministry. The church youth group reaching out to a fringe is not valued highly enough as a method of outreach.[20] In other situations this confusion is reversed: the nucleus group is seen as the only successful Christian approach to youthwork and incarnational ministry is rejected because it is not based in the church or because it is seen as a watering down of the gospel. The future of youth ministry in the church may well be secured only if we are able to articulate the difference between these two disciplines of youth ministry. Youthworkers themselves need to be clear what they are setting out to do and present their work honestly to the church as being either one or the other kind of approach. Training for youthwork needs also to embrace these distinctions and train people appropriately for their particular calling. In addition to this, those in the church making decisions about the direction of youthwork and the allocation of resources need to adopt this two-discipline framework in order that young people of all kinds have the gospel shared with them in the way which is most appropriate to their particular culture.

Questions to Ponder and Discuss

1. What is the Inside-Out approach? What is the Outside-In approach?

2. Do you agree with this Inside-Out and Outside-In distinction? Can you think of individual examples where each type has worked? Do you think one way is a better way to reach youth? In which of these ways do you personally prefer to minister?

3. How do you compare parachurch youth ministries with church youth ministries? What are the differences among Youth for Christ, Young Life, Campus Crusade, Fellowship of Christian Athletes, etc.? What are the advantages and disadvantages of such ministries outside the church? Can you get these organizations and church youth groups all together in your town or area? What would be the advantages of doing so?

4. To what extent can committed Christian young people reach their uncommitted friends? How can they be helped to do so? Are there young people at school or on the streets that Christian youth may not be able to bring in? Do you think the average high school student has the time, skills, and inclination to reach into subcultures radically different from his or her own? What could be done to make this sort of outreach work better?

5. How different are the subcultures of church kids and non-church kids? Can you think of any young people in your city or town who would not be

comfortable in your youth group? Might some of these outsiders make your members uncomfortable? What can be done about this?

6. How important is it for youth leaders to understand subcultures? What are the subcultures of young people that need to be reached by adult missionaries using a style of incarnational infiltration?

Chapter 2

A Theology
of Youth Ministry

here is a difference between a theology of youth ministry and a theology of young people. A theology of young people is based upon the insights, culture, and voices of particular groups of young people. It is when groups of young people begin to speak of their encounter with God that a theology which is "indigenous" to them begins to emerge. A theology of youth ministry on the other hand seeks to demonstrate how our understanding of God shapes and influences the practice of youth ministry. This chapter is an attempt to link what we believe as Christians—our theology—to what we do as youthworkers.

Youth Ministry and the Mission of God◆◆◆◆◆◆◆

We work among young people because of the God we believe in. The Bible speaks of a God who crosses boundaries to build relationship with people. This is the God of Abraham, Isaac, Jacob, and Moses. We see God in the burning bush, the still small voice, the vision in the temple and walking in the garden with Adam. This is the God we see assuming human form in the birth of Jesus. God accepts the limitations of our own nature in order that we might experience God's presence and love. At a wedding, sitting at a table, in stories, and through works of power we see God in Jesus walking beside the disciples. Ultimately this journey leads Jesus to death on the cross and his triumphant resurrection. At Pentecost the resurrected presence of God falls upon Jesus' followers. In community life, evangelism, and mission; through persecution, failure, loss, and suffering, the Spirit of God embraces people. Walking the way of Jesus becomes a Spirit-filled life of faith.

The Christian gospel tells the story of a missionary God.[1] Relationship is at the center of the being of God whom we know as Father, Son, and Holy Spirit: Creator, Redeemer, and Sustainer. We see the God who is three and who is one as God is revealed in mission. We know of God in no other way than as one who seeks humanity in relationship. It is this God who calls us and inspires us to reach out to young people. Youth ministry/Christian youthwork is therefore grounded in the missionary nature of God. The mission is God's, not ours. We are called and inspired by God to participate in seeking relationship with all human beings. Our practice as youthworkers finds its true rationale in the God who calls us to share God with young people.

The Practice of the Mission of God ◆◆◆◆◆◆◆◆◆

God seeks humanity because of a radical breakdown in relationship. People are created in the image of God. We bear the mark of the Creator. Male and female we reflect God's face and resonate to the Creator's voice. Our highest ideals and deepest desires rest on this foundation. We are who we are because of our createdness. But the biblical story pivots on the failure of humanity to respond to the voice of God. We are fallen, in rebellion, and in denial, distant from a God who calls us without being heard. We are sought by God who desires us and loves us. It is out of love that God calls us to turn and meet our Creator's embrace.

To be truly Christian, youthwork must carry within it the essential dynamic of the gospel story. We are called to proclaim this gospel in both our words and our deeds in ways that the young people can understand. The gospel story is rooted in God who is the same yesterday, today, and forever. This unchanging story, however, must be proclaimed afresh in each generation. Our task is to seek a location within the mindset and subculture of particular groups of young people where this story can come to life. The gospel is thus to be "incarnated" in the basic expressions, lifestyle, and accent of young people where it can bless, redeem, and transform individuals and communities. For some young people, the God who seeks us is first encountered when youthworkers and the church community show care and concern. The care we offer in the day-to-day activities of youthwork acts as a concrete prophetic sign of the God who desires relationship, but the gospel so lived out should also be spoken. We are called to tell the story of a God who seeks relationship, a God who calls young people to worship and service in his name. With some groups of young people the telling of the story will be the starting point of youthwork. The telling of the story, however, is then reinforced by the faithful lifestyles of youth ministers who act as mentors, as models, in the path of discipleship.

Youth ministry is shaped by our experience of the God who calls us to mission. We do youthwork as Christians for no other reason than that we tell the gospel story. We may wish to frame our practice in terms of educational theory, counselling, community work, sport and leisure provision, or any number of other theoretical models of working with young people, but to do so as Christian youthworkers is to seek to integrate these perspectives into the overarching nature of the larger gospel story. It is this commitment to the role of the gospel as the story within which our other commitments are understood and have meaning that brings an identity to the Christian youth minister/youthworker. When the relationship between the gospel and other theories of working with young people is reversed, the youthworker ceases to be Christian youthworker and becomes a youthworker or a community worker who happens to be Christian. For youthworkers involved in projects outside of a specifically Christian setting or funded by local authorities, such a self-understanding and identity may be a matter of course.

The Shape of the Gospel ♦♦♦♦♦♦♦♦♦♦♦♦♦♦♦♦♦

A theology of ministry must seek to be a distinctive expression of the gospel in the light of current social situations. The gospel story is characterized by polarities of emphasis which shape our practice. A distinctive contextualized theology of youth ministry will depend upon how we position ourselves in relation to: The incarnation and the cross, redemption and repentance, transcendence and immanence, hope of the kingdom, and the work of the Holy Spirit.

♦The Incarnation and the Cross

In the story of Jesus we see life and death, joy and suffering. To emphasize the incarnation of God as a human being is to affirm social life, the physical body, and human culture. The Jesus of the gospels is social. In Jesus we see someone who enjoys company, who is a guest at dinner parties, who is present at weddings. While John the Baptist is cast as the ascetic who rants in the desert, Jesus is accused of being a wine bibber and a friend of sinners. Jesus valued friendship highly; with Martha, Mary, and Lazarus we see a deep affectionate relationship emerge. Their grief becomes his own and forms the backdrop to the miracle of resurrection. The Jesus of the gospels is physical; he sleeps, eats, drinks. He gets tired, needs to rest, and finds the crowds a strain. In his resurrected glory he is still corporeal. "Put your hand in my side," he says to Thomas.[2] Children sit on his knee and the sick are healed by the touch of his hands. The incarnation locates the revelation of God in a specific time, place, and culture. Jesus was a Jew with a family, a tribe, a history, and an occupation. He spoke Aramaic and he knew the Hebrew scriptures, he was circumcised and an active participant in synagogue and temple worship.

When we turn to contemplate the cross of Christ we are confronted with self-denial and suffering. At Gethsemane Jesus is tormented with the prospect of what is ahead. Betrayed, abandoned, mocked, and scorned, Jesus is eventually hung up like a piece of meat and left to die. But the torment of the cross is perhaps only partially physical. "My God, my God, why have you forsaken me?" tells of a deeper anguish.[3] It is the Father who wills it and the Spirit who carries the power of it into the present, but this resolution of the Godhead leads down the path of a cosmic suffering. In an act of self-commitment to humanity and relationship the divine Trinity tears itself apart.[4] The way of mission inevitably leads to the cross. Jesus makes this very clear. To follow him is to embrace self-denial: "If any man would come after me, let him deny himself and take up his cross and follow me. For whoever would save his life will lose it; and whoever loses his life for my sake and the gospel's will save it."[5]

The incarnation and the cross of Christ are of course intimately connected in the gospel story. Yet in developing a theology for ministry these aspects of the story are experienced as contrasting points of attraction. Ministry which affirms life has to be balanced with self-sacrifice and asceticism. The joy of physicality and culture and creativity is to be tempered by a sense of discipline and the higher calling of commitment to God's work. Yet at the same time, sensible, measured, and temperate ministry is possibly not what is required. We are called to live lives of creative integrity. A prophetic witness in any culture will not be moderate; it will have to form itself around one of these polarities. Some will be called to the cross while others will seek to affirm life and engage in cultural creativity. The aesthetic and ascetic, the incarnation and the cross, will co-exist in the church. Yet in each case the one will always need the other. Those walking the way of the cross must always affirm the positive nature of human life. Those who are deeply incarnated in human life and society will at one time or another be called to self-denial and suffering.

Youthwork which is incarnational will see in the life of Jesus a model for ministry. It is essential, not only to good practice, but also to the proclamation of the gospel, that relationships are at the heart of the work. Dean Borgman says that we are called to "waste time" with young people, "hanging out" with them.[6] Unprogammed social time will form the heart of our ministry, as it seems to have done in the life of Jesus. Young people will learn to become Christian because they are in regular informal contact with Christian people who model the faith. The dilemmas and challenges of Christian discipleship will be dealt with while we are on the move from one informal activity to another: car journeys, conversations while going fishing, coffee in the kitchen, a postcard sent from a trip abroad. The substance of incarnational ministry is the valuing of contact between adults and young people in the everyday and ordinary things of life. Friendship and relationship will not only be the means of ministry, it will be the ministry itself.

Youthwork which is incarnational must affirm the physicalness of life. Growth in body and mind characterize adolescence. Sex and sexuality are the key issues which young people are faced with in the teenage years. Christian youthwork cannot afford to locate itself in the midst of adolescence without a creative contribution to the storm which surrounds sexual identity and sexual behavior. Unfortunately we inherit a Christian tradition which has seen in the cross of Christ a reason to chastise the flesh, deny passion, and ignore the body. Our bodies may well be seen as temples of the Holy Spirit, but the emphasis has tended to rest most heavily on Spirit rather than body. The incarnation indicates the sacredness of the physical body as a vessel worthy of God's indwelling. Youth culture celebrates the body, and the Christian faith incarnated among young people must find appropriate ways to affirm this. Youth ministry contextualized in youth culture will see physicality and image transformed in God's sight. Our worship and our expression of fellowship must be both "carnal" and Holy. We need to affirm the image of God not as a disconnected "Spirit" within young people, but as a renewed vision of the way that God sees us. At the same time, in a culture where style and image are the highest ideal, the cross of Christ may act as a rebuke. We can sell out to relevance, we can drown our faith in culture. The cross of Jesus calls us to prize costly relationship above product. Being on the cutting edge of youth ministry means that you bleed for others, not for art.

♦Redemption and Repentance

The gospel story pivots on the significance of the cross. The cross reveals the hidden passion of God for humanity. Father, Son, and Holy Spirit break their own fellowship to restore fellowship with humanity. The cross is a cosmic enacting of the desire God has for renewed relationship with his creation. A theology of salvation which makes sense of the cross is not an optional extra for Christian youthworkers. The centrality of the death of Christ for the gospel story means that this event must be right at the heart of our practice. Faith in the saving death of Christ is not a personal conviction or peculiar evangelical bent. The death of God the Son for us must make a difference to the way we relate to young people. If we do not see how the cross might be of central significance in our work, then we are probably less than we should be as Christian youthworkers. The themes of redemption and repentance act as bridges between the lives of young people and the centerpiece of the Christian story.

The cross is central to the New Testament. There are a number of metaphors, however, which are used to tell the significance of the event.[7] The idea of redemption or ransom is one of these. Rather than a full blown explanatory theory of how the death of Christ brings about salvation, the word redemption offers a snapshot or word picture of the significance of the cross. The New Testament picture of redemption is drawn from the world of the marketplace and commerce. In this environment someone or something is "redeemed" when it has been bought back.[8] The image may well be of a slave who is bought back and then set free. "In him we have redemption through his blood, the forgiveness of our trespasses, according to the riches of his grace."[9]

As the Anglican liturgy puts it, "He opened wide his arms for us on the cross; he put an end to death by dying for us."[10] The love of God seen in the death of Christ invites a response. Though once far off and neglectful of a relationship with the divine, we are called by the passion of God to respond. We are facing away, but we turn to be greeted by our maker. From a journey of independence and rebellion we retrace our steps and meet the love of God full on at the foot of the cross. It is of the essence of the gospel story that Christ's death effects a change in people. "When I survey the wondrous cross on which the prince of glory died, my richest gain I count but loss and pour contempt on all my pride."[11] We are the returning son of the parable finding in our desperation a father who has waited day after day at the end of the drive to embrace us and take us home.

Redemption and repentance signify the dynamic of the narrative flow of the Christian story. Repentance brings a resolution, where the estranged actors in the story eventually meet. The loving self-giving on the part of God is completed by its acknowledgement by humanity. Love is returned with love in relationship. But to turn away from the outpouring of divine passion leads to isolation and death. Christian youthwork will locate itself within this dynamic of redemption and repentance. Each young person will be seen as being of infinite worth because of the price that has been paid for his or her freedom in the death of Christ. The self-worth and self-identity which young people are seeking to achieve will be respected but interpreted within the context of the overarching story of the gospel. Without returning to God, life remains hollow, however creative, energetic, and positive it may be. God's passionate desire for relationship with every young person is the foundation stone of our ministry.

At the same time Christian youthworkers are called to respect and support young people whatever their response to the death of Christ. To do so is a sign of God's grace. Christ died for all and loves all. The Christian message is one of grace, before we respond. The dynamic of the gospel story has space within it for people to turn away from the passion of God. Youthwork should be characterized by a realistic and sympathetic understanding that this is the case. While repentance will form part of our desire for all people, the reality will be that some will choose to remain distant from their Creator. This choice must be respected.

Turning toward the light involves a turning away from darkness. In young people's lives that which binds them and holds them down may be drug abuse, social disadvantage, poverty, bullying, or any number of implacable problems. Christian youthwork will attempt to bring liberation and empowerment in these situations by offering counsel, support, and friendship. The day-to-day practical offer of care will be seen as a prophetic sign of redemption and repentance. When individual young people begin to turn and address their problems, when they cease to be victims and start to build lives full of self-confidence and creativity, the youthworker will understand his or her practice as the inbreaking of the kingdom of God. The young people may or may not acknowledge the divine drama which is being played out in their lives, but the youth-worker will see youthwork as an invitation for young people to respond to a God who continues to bleed for them, who waits for them and longs for them to come home.

Repentance will have an effect on every aspect of a young person's life. To turn to follow Christ is to set new priorities. When we see ourselves in the face of Christ on the cross, the story of God becomes our story, and life can never be the same. Our identity becomes transformed in a loving encounter with God. A change of identity is not to be confused with a change in social life or cultural appreciation. Coming to faith should not require that we substitute another culture for our culture, or another set of relationships for our social relationships. The Holy Spirit changes us to be more fully who we should be within the setting where we most naturally fit. But when we turn to God, some of our behaviors, attitudes, and values will become uncomfortable. We will begin to see the world through God's eyes. His concerns will become our concerns. The gospel demands that people change. An encounter with God brings renewal and challenge. Youth ministry without repentance is youth minis-try without God. This is not to say that we should necessarily expect young people who turn to Christ to readily fit the cul-turally conditioned mores of the church. The practical implica-tions of repentance will be played out within each subculture as the Holy Spirit leads young people in the way of Christ. We should expect repentance and change, but youth ministers may not be able to predict what this will look like unless they are closely involved with a particular group of young people.

♦Transcendence and Immanence

The Christian story tells of an unknowable God who makes himself known. We do not know God in the same way that we know about a part of his creation. We cannot make God the object of our study and enquiry. We know God as he chooses to come to us. We know God as we are caught up in his knowing of us. This aspect of Christian spirituality and experi-ence means that faith is always mystery and never certainty. It is the moment when we think that we have got God figured out that we have actually lost sight of him.[12]

Encounter with God is dangerous. The beginning of wisdom is the fear of God. God is not a casual acquaintance or a cuddly toy. The Creator of the world is not at our beck and call. We cannot summon God up in prayer or in worship. We encounter God because God chooses to meet with us. We give ourselves to God, we do not strike up a contract. We never meet God as equals. We do not possess or own the gospel story of which we are a part. We participate in the story as players and actors keeping in step with a God who knows the next scene. Worship is the act of acknowledging the godness of God and the creatureliness of humanity.

It is in the life of Christ that God is made most fully known. Faith therefore rests upon the revelation of God in Christ. We are able to encounter God in this revelation through the words of the New Testament. Our understanding of God therefore rests upon, and is judged by, the revelation of God contained within the Bible. All theology is an abstraction from the authoritative biblical material. All theology, however biblical, stands outside the gospel story and is provisional, only partially or temporarily true. All of our pictures of God, our habitual turns of phrase, and our cherished lines from choruses, teeter on the brink of idolatry, because to reduce God to our knowledge of him is to make of our theology an idol.[13]

The God of the gospel story is beyond knowing, transcendent. He is the creator, the alpha and the omega. He offers himself for our contemplation in the life, death, resurrection, and ascension of Christ. He meets us in a narrative, and true knowing can be found only in participation in the story. Our reflection on the biblical story, including this one, is an act of faithful engagement, a search for meaning. To make our theology into a search for objective truth is to move beyond the dynamic of faith.

Youth ministry is worked out within the context of the transcendence and the immanence of God. The youth minister will always be caught between the familiarity and the mystery of God. On the one hand there is a desire to invite young people to seek a God who can be known. On the other hand there should be a realization that all our knowing is to be treated carefully as an act of grace rather than a possession. The God we meet as friend and guide is also the God who is beyond comprehension and profoundly unknowable. We desperately want young people to have a meaningful faith, but we need to offer this possibility in a way which avoids idolatry. It is God who encounters young people in the midst of our programs, relationships, and spiritual activities. Our skill as youthworkers is empty without the work of the Holy Spirit. We will be tempted to guarantee encounter with God, but this we must resist. We will inevitably at times be drawn into an overreliance upon techniques. In our desire for success we will turn to the latest relevant approach to evangelism. In themselves these may be of considerable worth, but their rhetoric may fool us into seeing their application as essential or inevitable. It is God who seeks young people and chooses to call them to himself. Encounter with God is a spiritual event shrouded with mystery. Despite all of our efforts, training, and experience, we are powerless beside the sovereign choosing of God.

The search for an expression of the faith which makes sense to young people is basic to Christian youthwork. The desire to communicate carries with it the possibility of simplification. Adolescence can be a time where the world is painted in very strong colors. The subtleties of shade and hue are generally a characteristic of later life. Youth ministry has at times ill-served young people by portraying faith as clear-cut and matter-of-fact. The widespread absence of formal theological training for youth ministry means that Christian youthworkers are prone to the latest catchy trends. This has meant that the immanence of God has been emphasized at the expense of God's transcendence. The otherness of a God who is to be feared and respected has often been played down. The mystery of faith has been debunked, unpacked, demythologized, and illustrated into nonexistence. In our hands, the creator God who comes to judge the world has become a friend who is always by our side. Prayer is calling up God on the phone and worship is a "rave in the nave." Not that in themselves any of these expressions of the faith are wrong or mistaken: God is indeed a friend, prayer can be a time of "calling God up," and worship can be a dance celebration in the sanctuary. It is the reduction of the faith to these things and these things alone which needs to be questioned. When our simplifications leave young people with only part of the picture, is it any wonder that in later life they search for a more satisfying truth than that which they have found within the evangelical constituency?[14]

◆The Hope of the Kingdom

The kingdom of God was the central teaching of Jesus. He enters onto the scene in Mark's gospel proclaiming that the time is at hand: "repent and believe the Gospel."[15] The kingdom of God is ushered in with the presence of the incarnate Son of God. To be in the company of Jesus is to be close to the kingdom of God.[16] At the same time the kingdom is to be expected. We wait for the kingdom and pray for its fulfilment. The kingdom is about the end times. These end times are there in the life and death of Christ, but they are summed up in the eventual close of the age.

For the Christian the kingdom of God is about personal and community renewal in the present, and it is also about the assurance that God will see things put right in the future. Christian hope therefore is concerned with encounter with a liberating God who sets us free to see our present with new eyes and the future with expectation. The kingdom is about setting the prisoners free, preaching good news to the poor, and giving the blind sight. Hope is in the air, and the possibility of transformed lives is brought into reality by the death and resurrection of Christ. Repentance is turning to greet these promises as a reality which is both in the present and eventually to be fulfilled in the future.

Christian youthworkers are called to be heralds of this kingdom. Our feet are blessed as we carry good news to those we meet. We are torch bearers charged with keeping our lights shining so that others may see. Spirituality is the basic ingredient of our work, whatever discipline of youth ministry we practice. Our prayer and reflection upon the Bible and daily life is in no way marginal to our effectiveness as youthworkers. It is the expected and fulfilled hope of the kingdom which gives us the energy to interact with young people and with community groups. The kingdom of God is a vision which we see in outline in the changed lives, expectations, and choices which emerge in young people's lives through our work. The kingdom is what keeps us in the action as we wait expectantly for what God has promised to bring about.

To be a Christian youthworker is therefore to be a worker for the kingdom of God. The concerns of the kingdom are to become our concerns. Social inequality, economic hardship, racial prejudice, sexual discrimination, physical disability, emotional distress, educational disadvantage therefore rightly fall within our purview. These issues are spiritual issues in that they are an offense to the kingdom of God. The secular youth service may share some of these concerns, but their agenda is not synonymous with ours. The Christian youthworker is a servant of the kingdom of God rather than a particular political or social agenda. To the extent that the desire of God for justice and equality coincides with the programs of secular youthwork we are in accord, but this is not to say that Christian youthwork is anything other than a theologically informed and understood framework. It is the message of the kingdom, not the insistence of secular philosophy, which reminds us that God is concerned with the whole of life.

The Christian youthworker looks back to the cross of Christ, engages in the mission of God in the present, and looks for liberation in the future. The dynamic of the now-but-not-yet kingdom determines our practice as youthworkers. Our ministry is shaped by the need for a vision of hope among young people, hope which rests on what God has done in Christ, what he is doing in the present, and what he will do at the end of the age. This is kingdom hope, and it is expressed better than I am able by a meditation on hope which was written for a JOY service in Oxford.

> Some people say—life is a circle—
> you're born—you grow up—you work—
> you grow old—you die.
>
> Some people say—what will be, will be.
>
> Some people say, "There are no jobs
> so no one will want me."
> Some people say, "There will always
> be war—
> what can I do about it?"
> Some people say, "There will always be homelessness—
> tis a shame."

Some people say, "The world's a terrible place
and I want no part in it."
Some people say—"Who knows what my life will be like
tomorrow, I'll just wait and see."

Hope says "Bullshit."

Hope helps you see a different reality,
a world where anything is possible
not just for tomorrow but for today.

Hope helps you see, not just what things could be like
but what today is like
in a different light.

Hope is not an empty promise
or a dream of escaping.

Hope changes the color of
the world we live in.

Hope changes our faces from
the faces of the bored and the defeated
to the faces of those who
see life as an adventure.

Life requires risk, experiment,
adventure, possibility.
In short,
life requires hope.

If there's no hope, there's no point.
With God there's never no point.[17]

◆The Work of the Holy Spirit

The Holy Spirit is an active partner with the Father and
the Son in every part of the gospel story. The Spirit is there
moving across the waters; it is by means of the Spirit that the
stuff of life is changed and brought into being. As the Spirit de-

scends upon Jesus at his baptism, we are given a privileged glimpse into the creative energy of communication which flows between the Father and the Son. The life of Jesus is one which is worked out in fellowship and with the energy and activity of the Holy Spirit. At Pentecost the Holy Spirit descends upon the disciples in tongues of fire. They begin to speak in languages other than their own, and as they preach the gospel, works of wonder and the Spirit's power characterize their witness. God is three and God is also one. The Holy Spirit does not just appear at the end of the story to bless the church. The Holy Spirit, with the Father and the Son, plays a fully scripted role in every aspect of the story.

The advent of the Charismatic movement and recent new waves of God's blessing have tended to confuse the youthwork situation. There are many points of difference between Christian churches concerning the action of the Holy Spirit. My own view is that these differences are something to be celebrated and enjoyed. It is the distinctive elements in spirituality and Christian worship which tend to hold my fascination. Those things which we hold in common are extremely important, but when worship and spiritual life are reduced to these things alone, the result tends to leave me a little cold. A theology of youth ministry needs to draw upon the breadth of our present understanding of God. At the same time we need to be critical of our tribal affiliations, especially when they are espoused with seemingly very little reflection or self-criticism.

One of the key questions in Christian youthwork concerns the means by which young people are changed by their encounter with God. Youth ministry has developed three separate lines of thought on this issue. Each of us will tend to favor one of these approaches over the others, and our ministry will be shaped by this understanding of change.

the Holy Spirit changes people

The fully blown charismatic tendency is to turn at every occasion to miraculous intervention. The techniques and skills of youth ministry are thus regarded as being somewhat unspiritual and basically irrelevant. According to this view, the crucial thing is that we worship God and we invite the Spirit to come and meet us. Stories from this approach to youth ministry tend to emphasize the unintentional nature of God's miraculous intervention. Despite our lack of knowledge of what is happening in a young person's life, the Spirit has led us to pray the right prayer or say the right prophetic words. At the same time evangelism can be reduced to involvement in worship. If we can get the non-Christians into the worship service, then they will encounter God with power and that will change them.

the word changes people

In response to the growth in charismatic spirituality, conservative evangelicalism has tended to become more strident. In contrast to a Spirit-led miraculous expectation, these Christians emphasize the importance of the preaching of the word. The view is that the Christian gospel is essentially a message to which young people need to listen and respond. The key to successful and faithful Christian youthwork is therefore the presentation of truth. The gospel can be expressed in a set of propositions which are to be treated as absolute objective truth.

Young people are changed by hearing the word of God and responding to what they hear. The word of God must be accepted, and human sin and inadequacy must be acknowledged as a block to the successful working of grace in our lives. This process is from beginning to end a rational discourse. Preaching is a means of sharing ideas concerning God. Young people for their part must respond to these ideas by coming to terms, rationally, with their own sinfulness. Commitment therefore becomes a matter of deciding to follow Christ.

young people are changed through youthwork as process

For many Christians the practice of youthwork has meant the discovery of particular approaches to informal education, community work, empowerment, or counselling theory. Drawing on methodologies for social and individual change, Christians have adopted and adapted these practices. Change, according to these procedures, depends upon the energy of individuals and communities to set about changing themselves. Youthwork will aim to provide a forum within which young people will gain an increased understanding of their own situation and the wider society. The Christian youthworker will set these issues within the context of the work of God in the world. It is when the Spirit of God begins to move young people to demand change in their own lives and at a grass roots level in this community that the kingdom comes into being. The key to this will be young people discovering their own ability to change.

These three portraits are of course caricatures. Youthworkers in practice will adopt any of these approaches, or more than one at the same time. But whatever approach or combination of approaches is adopted, there is a need for a theological reflection upon the action and work of the Holy Spirit to inform the work.

The Spirit, as we have seen, is involved with all aspects of the gospel story. Creation is brought about by the action of the Spirit. This means that we must not play down the ability of young people to discover their own power. We are powerful and able to change because God has made us that way. The natural abilities of people are blessed by God's Spirit in the supernatural but also in natural ways. To regard insights and styles of work which are based on theories of individual and social change as somehow "unspiritual" is to ignore the breadth of the Spirit's engagement with the world. At the same time those Christians committed to community work or informal education will need to develop an understanding of how God is at work in this process if it is to be understood as truly Christian. To admit the involvement of the Holy Spirit in social and individual change must leave us open to the supernatural, or the "charismatic." The Spirit moves in creation through both the natural and the supernatural. We cannot have one without the other. A Spirit who does not work wonders is less than God.

A theology of the word is essential. The word of God in Christian tradition has been regarded as the means by which God effects change in the world. It is the word of God in Isaiah which does not return without bringing into reality the wish of God. Evangelicals see the preaching of the word as the means by which people "hear the good news." Hearing the good news is essential to spiritual renewal.[18] Evangelicalism has grown and developed out of this understanding of spiritual change. We need to affirm that the gospel story speaks of a historic reality and that it is possible to speak with truth about the death of Jesus and humanity's need for repentance. The Holy Spirit is deeply involved with this process. It is the Spirit who is sent out in order that the death of Christ can become a reality in people's lives. For it is through the Spirit that we experience grace. The Spirit quickens our hearts to respond as we ought to the gift of life. Yet the Spirit also is at work through the human techniques and insights of youth ministry. To focus exclusively upon the reception of the word of God as the means of learning and change is to reduce the Spirit and make of our understanding and hearing an idolatry. Similarly the miraculous and powerful intervention of God in our lives must not be discounted or put down. The God of the gospel story is disruptive and disturbing. He is not reducible to a set of objective absolutes. The charismatic intervention of the Spirit speaks of the ability of God to defy our neat categories.

The energy and life which is sweeping through charismatic congregations and churches at the present time is extremely exciting. Our enthusiasm for the dramatic intervention of God in the lives of young people is well founded, but we need to allow for the possibility that the Holy Spirit is broader than the purely miraculous. While encounter with God in worship and in ministry is profound and valuable, youth ministry from within the charismatic tradition needs to take the process of education, growth, and development among young people seriously. The Holy Spirit in the gospel story interacts with creation without doing violence to its essence. Creation is brought into being through the activity of the Spirit. This perspective needs to temper the enthusiasm for the miraculous among charismatic groups. Similarly, the realization that it is not only possible but can be "Spirit inspired" to think rationally about the Christian faith, must not be lost in the current scene.

Questions to Ponder and Discuss

1. What is the difference between a theology of youth ministry and a theology of young people? How does a theology of young people develop? How are the contents of this chapter different than a theology of young people?

2. Do you agree that Christian theologies can have important differences in style and emphasis—along with faithful agreement to the living and written words of God?

3. What are some of the main features of the theology developed in this chapter?

4. Why is the gospel so central to a theology of youth ministry? Why is the incarnation so central to a theology of youth ministry? What are some of the implications of the incarnation to our theology and to our ministry?

5. How is the atonement presented here? Can the cross be central in an incarnational theology? Is the repentance of a young person different from that of other people?

6. What do we have to know and feel about young people today to understand the importance of hope in the Christian gospel and youth ministry? How deeply do we need to experience the opposite of hope in order to understand young people today?

7. What do you think about the relative emphases on the Holy Spirit and the objective word of God in youth ministry?

The *Incarnational* Approach

Relationships are the fuel on which youthwork travels. For the nucleus model the relational energy which makes the approach work is primarily supplied by young people who share their faith with their friends. In the incarnational approach relationships are also very much to the fore. In this case however we are talking of the relationship between Christian adults and young people. This chapter explores how relationships between young people and youth ministers change and develop as ministry among unchurched young people evolves. A pattern for working Outside-In is presented. In the last part of the chapter these insights are applied to work which is Inside-Out.

To be engaged in building relationships with young people is an intentional activity. We choose to move outside of what we would consider our usual friendship groups and social contacts to make a connection with young people. Our presence among a group of young people is an "intervention" in that we have crossed a natural social boundary in order that we might bring about change in the lives of young people. We might understand this change as empowerment, or helping, or even in more social terms as building relationships, or we might express our reasons for crossing the boundary as having to do with a desire to share the Christian faith. However we express our motivation for doing youthwork, we must accept the inevitable artificiality of what we are doing. Given the normal course of events, we would not make such intimate connections with a group of young people. The only reason we are in relationship is that we are Christian youthworkers; i.e., we believe that we have been called by God to engage in sharing the gospel. The incarnational discipline of youth ministry, like any other approach to youthwork, needs to recognize that it is an activity which is out of the ordinary. It is for this reason that it is imperative that we are clear in our own minds what exactly we are involved in. Chapter 2 explored the theology of youthwork. This provides a set of values and some idea of the style of our involvement with young people. In addition to this there is also a need to be able to express a basic plan as to how we envisage our work among young people growing and developing into the future. Without such a plan we are likely to run afoul of several problems which are often associated with youthwork.

First we could very easily lose our way in the work we are doing. A lack of direction in the work will not only mean that we will be unsuccessful in being good news among young people, it could also mean that we disappoint those who support our work. If we are voluntary or full-time workers we owe a duty to those who pray for our work or to the local church which encourages us to work with young people. If we are able to express our aims and objectives clearly, then those around us are able to hold us accountable for the progress of the work and we are also able to assess how we are doing. Secondly, if we are clear in our own minds how we hope to see the work develop, then we will be less vulnerable to the influence that our own personality will have upon the work. Youthwork must be "safe"; i.e., we must remain certain that we are not engaging in youthwork primarily to satisfy our own need for sexual fulfilment, emotional security, power, or significance. Youth ministers are called to be good news among young people, not bad news.

We are bad news when our own lack of self-awareness leads us to abuse young people emotionally, physically, or spiritually. The key to avoiding such abuse will lie primarily in our own integrity and in a context in which we are held to account by people with whom we talk through what we do in the work. Every youthworker should have an agreed pattern of supervision for the work they are doing with young people. Patterns of supervision vary from organization to organization. For the purposes of this discussion, however, the key point is that all workers, voluntary or full-time, must have a formal contract to meet with a suitably qualified supervisor on a regular basis. This kind of supervision is a basic requirement of any work with young people. Alongside supervision we also need to keep in mind an agreed pattern for the work.[1]

A plan will help to identify when our own issues, needs, and personality are starting to pull the ministry out of line. The realistic youth minister will admit that it is not a question of "if," it is more likely to be matter of when or how disastrously we go out of line. Supervision and an agreed plan for the work are necessary because we are engaged in complicated relationships which will from time to time need to be adjusted or brought back into line. Thirdly we need to create a pattern for our ministry so that we are able to include others in the work. Youth ministry requires a team approach. In the first instance we may well have to start building relationships with young people on our own or in pairs. As the work progresses, however, it is vitally important that the number of adults involved in the work, either as volunteers, or as paid workers, is increased. Youth ministry which speaks of Jesus must model the community of faith. Young people in order to receive the fullness of the gospel need to see faith as living reality in a number of different people's lives. A clear plan for the work enables others to understand how the work is going to progress. They can get a grip on how their part in the work might develop and how this links with the role they are playing at the present time. The plan also enables them to value the parts of the work with which they are not directly concerned. They are therefore more able to see the work as whole and share in the overall vision.

A Model for Relational Outreach◆◆◆◆◆◆◆◆◆◆◆◆◆◆

The following pattern for working Outside-In is based upon my own experience among young people in Oxford. The model is a summary of the different approaches to youthwork which have been developed by myself and others in Oxford Youth Works. After several years of experimenting with various approaches to youthwork we have tried to sum up our work in five basic stages.[2] These five stages are a simplification of the route we have actually taken over the years. They are by no means a foolproof guarantee of success. Neither are they an infallible or unchangeable pattern of work. Rather they are regarded by myself and the others in the team at Oxford Youth Works as a measure or a guide for our work. We use this pattern as a starting point for our own creative attempts to reach out to young people. We have never wanted to feel that we are simply following a blueprint. In general we feel that the best youthwork has yet to be done.[3] In setting out this pattern I would therefore request that you attempt to treat the ideas in the same spirit. To the extent that it rings true, then take it as guide; to the extent that it seems off kilter, feel free to treat it as a starting point for you to do something which is more in keeping with your own situation.

The Five Stages of the Relational Model ◆◆◆◆◆◆

Each of the five stages is described below in terms of an answer to a question, how relationships between young people and youthworkers grow, a program of activities, and a spiritual challenge.

◆Contact

When I was working as church-based youthworker I was acutely aware that the young people I was meeting on a regular basis were all Christians. The structure of youth group meetings provided me with the only place where I met any young people at all. If a non-Christian came to the group, then I could welcome them and try to get to know them. If for long periods none came, then I was evangelistically rather dormant. One solution was to try to encourage the group to invite their friends along by running a "mission." This strategy, however, seemed to still rely upon the Christian young people's attracting their friends. Unfortunately my experience was that they seemed unwilling, or unable, to attract non-Christians into the group. The nucleus approach was not working (or at least that was my perception at the time); what could I do? Was there a way of working which did not depend upon the group of young people who had grown up in the church?

The question I started with was, "How can I meet non-Christian young people?" The solution I quickly came to was that in order to meet groups of young people I would have to find a way of going to the places where they naturally "hung out." My first choice was the local school. As a full-time youthworker I was available to visit at lunch times. Through previous visits to the school I was aware that at that time there was a thriving culture of teenage bands. Music was one of my interests, so I devised a plan to get to know these pupils who were trying to get going in the music scene in Oxford. My plan was relatively simple. I went to the school and did an assembly. Working with the blessing of the music teacher and the Headmaster, I asked anyone interested in learning to play guitar, bass, or drums to meet me at break time in the hall. I also offered to come and meet up with any pupils who were starting to get bands together. That break time I was swamped by young people all wanting to get going with learning to be rock stars. In addition to the large group of beginners, there were also three young bands who came by to check me out. Over the next few weeks I tried to get to as many band rehearsals as I could. In addition to this I opened up a room at the school and got going with some basic guitar instruction.

My answer to the question, "How can I meet young people?" is "one at a time." I know of a place where for the last few years a group of volunteers have been going into the town center on weekday nights to meet the young people who gather there. This is not a hard or tough city center but a small town, where local young people who are at loose ends drift into the deserted neighborhoods when they are too young to hang out in cars or get into pubs. Over a period of years these youth-workers have built caring and supportive relationships with these young people, acting as resources for advice and support at times of crisis. In recent times one of the young people has started to come along to church through the work of the group.

Sports are another good way to meet young people. There are many Christians who are deeply involved in the lives of young people because they are regularly acting as coaches with sports teams. A group called Christians in Sport, which is similar to the Fellowship of Christian Athletes, developed an approach to relationship-based outreach in which Christian adults already involved in sports—as coaches, players, etc.— build on those relationships.[4]

In many places groups of young people are all too evident. Some youthwork projects are started by churches because they can see that there are groups of young people hanging around on the streets, or even in the grounds of the church. Finding these young people may not be the problem, but there is still the question, "How do I get to meet them?" Groups of young people do appear to be threatening or just a little unnerving to the average adult. The thought of going up to a group of young people outside McDonalds is a very scary prospect. Contact work, however, is about the attitudes and skills which are necessary to move out from the relatively comfortable world of church-based youthwork into the ebb and flow of young people's lives.[5] For some of us this will mean finding shared activities or interests where we can start to build friendships with young people. For others of us it will mean finding ways to meet young people on the streets, in the shopping center, or in the local parks. However we develop contact, the aim will be to build long-term relationships.

Contact is the very first stage in a complicated process of relationship-based youthwork. At its simplest level contact is the time when you first connect with the group. To make contact successfully we have to journey onto the territory of a group of young people. This means finding a place where a group of young people are at home and comfortable and going to that place to be with them. Most adult encounters with young people take place in a social context where the young people are at a disadvantage to the adults. The role and authority we have as adults generally safeguard us from exposure to the real social world of young people. When adults arrive on young people's territory they often do so to tell them off or get them to clear out. Contact involves us in coming into social contact with individuals or groups of young people in ways that lay aside the normal adult authoritarian roles. We attempt to connect with young people in ways that do not impose our rules or guidelines upon them. Our first concern is that we are able to make a genuine connection which is based upon mutual respect and trust.

The starting point for this relational youthwork involves an uncritical position on the part of the adult youthworker. This does not mean that we will suspend our values or commitments as Christians. It means that when we first make connection with a group of young people we accept them as they are. We are the visitors in their world, and we will need to learn the correct way to relate. Our first priority is gaining some familiarity with the unwritten rules which govern the life of the group. We need to understand how the group works, who the leaders are, and who are the followers. Our starting point therefore must be one of being around the young people without trying to impose our values upon them. At times their behavior may cause us some embarrassment or even place us in a compromising position morally or legally. It is our task to maintain relationship but to do so without losing our integrity as youthworkers or as Christians. This will mean that during the early stages of contact work there may be occasions when we will have to leave the group. At other times we will have to decide what kind of compromise we are willing to make in order to maintain relationship.

Contact work is first and foremost about spending time with a particular group of young people. The worker will need to make a regular commitment to building relationships. The frequency of meetings will, to some extent, depend upon the amount of time the young people themselves spend together. A football team which meets twice a week will require the worker to make contact on at least one of these meetings. A group in school which is together every break and lunch time each school day will require at least three visits a week. The key is that enough time is spent in contact with the group so that the worker can become accepted as a regular and welcome visitor.

The youth minister needs to bear in mind at all times that he or she is engaged in building relationships as an adult. It is not our aim to become one of the gang. To seek acceptance as one of the guys or the girls is to defeat the object of our involvement. We are engaged in building relationships precisely because as adults we have something which is extremely valuable to offer to young people—i.e., friendship with a caring adult. If we sell out on our adultness in any way, we lose our greatest asset.

Contact ministry is primarily about a low level engagement with a group of young people. The main activity involves being around the young people as they do the things which make up their everyday lives. It is hardly necessary to say terribly much. A relationship can start with nod of a head or a smile. This however needs to lead on to more extended conversations as these seem appropriate. It is very important not to try too hard. Artificial interaction is forced and comes over as adult control. We have the purpose of getting to know these young people, but they may very well not share this agenda with us. We need to wait and hang about until the friendliness or curiosity of the group allows us to say something.

For those youth ministers involved in sporting, artistic, or musical activities, the same kind of rules apply. When I was helping young people learn the guitar, I saw it as being very important that I kept my organization of the activity to a minimum. The aim was to allow the young people space to get on with playing the instruments themselves. I would help out where I could, but on the whole I was just hanging around. I would wait for a chance to make conversation which came from the initiative of the young people themselves. Of course I had to keep a friendly and open manner. Silence can be very intimidating. The occasional encouraging comment went a long way. I have to say that when it comes to contact work, there can be a marked difference in working with boys or with girls. Youth ministers who work with groups of girls seem to strike up significant relationships much more quickly. One reason for this is that conversation and the exchange of information can be much more free flowing with girls than with boys.

Contact work is not for everyone. Making a connection with a group of young people outside of a formal youthwork setting can be very demanding. A good rule of thumb for anyone considering this work is the level of sociability that is part of their everyday lives. If they are the kind of people who find themselves in conversation with people at the supermarket checkout or waiting to buy a ticket for the train, then they are naturals for a detached pattern of contact work. If conversations happen best when they are engaged in a shared activity with people, then a more formal setting may be more suited to their personality.

Entering the social world of a group of young people is a spiritual journey. Youthwork therefore needs to start with a commitment to prayer and a belief that God is guiding the youthworker in the relationships being built. Prayer is therefore the basis for Christian youth ministry.

The acceptance which is a vital part of this first stage of work means that the youth minister should be continually looking for the way that God is leading in relationships. This demands a spiritual insight into the way that the relationship develops. All the time the need for friendship will need to be tempered by a concern to remain faithful to Christian belief. Above all it is the Holy Spirit who opens doors into relationship with young people. Fundamental to the approach must be the realization that we do not take the Spirit to these young people. God is intimately aware of the young people's lives and he is already at work among them. The youthworker is a concrete sign of God's interest and presence. It is therefore vital to be spiritually in touch with a God whose nature is to reach out to young people.

Contact work takes the youth minister outside the prescribed arena of church-based work. Suddenly it is not at all clear what the rules are. The worker is now a beginner learning the ropes. The experience of worship in church and even as youthworkers is no preparation for this kind of freewheeling role. Relationship with God is the key element in the work. In the first instance this means a commitment to search the scriptures continually for signs of how to engage in the lives of particular groups of young people we have come to know. The questions which the ministry raises need to be brought to the study of the Bible. This will sometimes mean that we search wider than the familiar proof text territory we may have been used to.

Setting out to meet young people should not be a lone ranger ministry. The youthworker is ministering among young people as part of the church. Every youthworker should therefore try to have a group of Christians who pray about the work. The group should serve as people who share the fears, frustrations, joys, and successes of the work. This kind of fellowship expresses the ownership of the whole church of this aspect of mission in a local area. A praying group also contributes to an atmosphere of spiritual energy and accountability for the work.

◆Extended Contact

Contact ministry is the bedrock upon which incarnational work is based. There is no substitute for being around young people on their own territory. The first stage of the work, however, should not be regarded as a temporary fishing trip to get something going with the group of young people. Neither should it be seen as the whole of the work.

In some places churches and youthworkers have invested heavily in finding ways to meet young people. Purchasing a minivan, building a gym, sponsoring a basketball league, or starting a coffeehouse or a game room have been ways that Christians have sought to develop contact with young people. The problem in some of these cases is that the work has not managed to move beyond the first level of relationship building. Conversations between workers and young people can remain on a fairly superficial level. The result is that intimacy and sharing has sometimes failed to materialize. This may be due to a high turnover of young people. An example of this would be a ministry based on a coffeehouse that is held in a church recreation room every other Saturday night. This kind of ministry may suffer from the infrequency with which individual young people drop by the coffeehouse. A young person who has appeared social one week might be unfriendly the next or more likely not even show up. A similar problem can arise when volunteer workers are not able to consistently be at all the coffeehouses. In this case, the likelihood that significant relationships will be formed is very low.

Extended contact is therefore a stage in the work that addresses the question, "How can relationships between workers and young people deepen?" Friendship happens as people do things together. When we share experiences we develop intimacy. The key to moving beyond the first stages of contact will therefore be finding a natural and mutually rewarding way to spend more time with the young people. It is essential that the youth minister does not try to rush this stage of the work. There is no shortcut to developing a trusting and mutual relationship with a group of young people. The clue to when it is right to try to move relationships forward will always come from the young people themselves. It could be that they themselves issue an invitation. For instance, after long weeks continually discussing baseball with a group the youthworker may well find himself or herself invited to go along to the next game. In some cases the youthworker may initiate the visit. When the group starts to discuss the forthcoming game, the youthworker could ask if it is okay to come along.

Extended contact moves a relationship physically away from the point of contact. This means that the group who meet at the mall go on a trip to the beach. The group who sits in the classroom goes to Pizza Hut after school. By being willing to do something with a group, the worker is signalling that the group members are significant. The young people for their part are expressing an acceptance of the youth minister that goes beyond the casual meeting which has so far characterized the work. They may feel that the youthworker has so far been just passing by, but now they are opened to new possibilities. From a closed horizon contact situation the work has opened up to seem full of possibilities.

Doing things with young people is not an end in itself. It is a means to deepen relationships. In the first instance this will come about because of shared experience. A good time will most likely be remembered by all concerned. But perhaps more significantly, extended contact allows for the young people and the youth minister to get to know each other better. Conversations are sparked in the minivan or on the bus. Suddenly the worker is able to speak at more length with individuals. The realization that the youth minister is committed to the group will often spark questions. "Why do you do this?" "Are you married?" "How come you work for a church? Do you believe it all then?" "What if we came to church? Would they like us?" These kinds of conversations are the initial stages in a deepening relationship. They are generally not a challenge, but a genuine enquiry. The youthworker finds herself being checked out concerning most aspects of her life, from sex, to drug taking, from where she lives and with whom, to what music she likes and why she wears such terrible clothes! For the youthworker the period of extended contact provides the space to get a little deeper with individuals and the group as a whole. Direct questions may be inappropriate, but there will be a need to go with the flow of what individuals bring up in conversations. The early stages of any conversation offer clues as to what we find important and what we would want to talk about more. It is the sensitive youthworker who follows these clues without putting people on the spot.[6]

Extended contact really can be anything. The keys will be that it is something which interests the young people concerned and that it allows for some kind of deeper sharing. Some activities, however, are of very limited worth (e.g., a rock concert). In my experience a visit to a rock concert with young people can be quite frustrating. There is little which can be shared when all you can do is yell as loud as you can into each other's ears because the band has cranked up the amps and is going at it full tilt. Nevertheless, the trip to the concert and after it (if you can still hear) can be extremely valuable. The concert gives a point of departure for conversation and a sense of having done something together.

Activities with young people fall into two kinds of groups. The first will be those situations where the group has decided to do something and the youthworker simply joins in. For instance, a group may decide to meet at the mall on a Saturday and check out the stores, other kids, etc. The youthworker may agree to be there and go along with the flow of the group's activities. In this situation the youthworker, while being an adult in the group, is not acting as organizer or "in loco parentis" (in place of parents). The status of this activity means that when problems arise the youthworker is not responsible in a technical sense; however, the adult will be expected to behave responsibly. For instance, on a trip to the mall it might become apparent that some of the group are shoplifting or intending to shoplift. In this situation the first thing to bear in mind is that an adult accompanying the group has a responsibility to take some action. This probably does not mean turning the young people in to the security people at the store or reporting them to the police. Relationship should be maintained, while it is made clear that the youthworker cannot have anything to do with stealing. This is an appeal for the young people to understand that as an adult the youthworker has responsibilities and values. The youthworker is not saying, "shoplifting is wrong, therefore you must stop doing it." The youthworker *is* saying, however, "shoplifting is wrong, and for my sake please don't do it." This is an appeal to relationship. If the relationships with the group are not strong, then the youthworker will not be successful. If contact work has been going on for a while, then the young people will be more likely to value the relationship with the adult and they will realize that what they are doing is "out of order." If the group is not willing to accept the youth minister's advice, as a last resort the youthworker must leave the group to do what they have decided to do. It is important that the youthworker takes time to explain the reason for this action.

There is a most important distinction to be made between a trip organized by a youthworker and an informal joint activity. The former involves a great deal more responsibility on behalf of the youthworker and an acceptance of the youthworker in that role on the side of the young people. This development represents a quantum leap in relationship. For the youthworker the shift is from informal hanging around a group, accepting the general flow of behavior, the language, and the rules of the group, to becoming an adult who dictates what the ground rules of the trip will be. For instance, a trip in a minivan to the beach involves a number of responsibilities on the side of the youthworker which means that they cannot "go with the flow." A trip of this sort with young people who are under the age of eighteen requires some kind of parental consent. This might mean a visit to young people's homes to make sure that their parents or guardians are willing for them to come on the day trip. Insurance will generally mean that some kind of form is filled out. The youth minister will also have to follow the health and safety guidelines laid down by the supporting organization, the local authority, or the church from whom the minivan is hired.

The basic responsibilities involved in organizing a trip are an indication of a change in role for the youthworker, but more significantly the young people will need to come to terms with this new side to the youthworker's presence among them. A trip organized by the youthworker places the adult in the role of rule maker. For instance, there is the question of the minivan. The worker cannot allow the bus to be trashed. The question of smoking on the bus may be raised. The car rental company or the local church may have made it clear to the youth minister that smoking in the bus is not allowed. A crucial transition from contact ministry to extended contact work can be brought about by this kind of question. The youth-worker has to act as a responsible adult and stick to the rules of hiring the minivan and risk the disapproval of the group. The only way forward is for the youthworker to negotiate with the young people. In many cases it is essential to discuss issues such as the problem of smoking in the minivan with the group before the trip ever gets underway. The conversation could go something like this.

> Youthworker: "There's a problem. We are not allowed to smoke on the minivan."

> Young People: "What?"

> Youthworker: "Sorry, it's the church's minivan, and they don't want it to smell like an ashtray on Sunday when they pick up the old folks."

> Young People: "Couldn't we smoke out the window? We could clear it up afterwards and spray some air freshener."

> Youthworker: "Look, I promised the guy at the church no smoking and I don't want to let him down. What I thought is we could take a cigarette break halfway, what do you think?"

These kinds of discussions are the stuff of which youth-work is made.[4] Without these kinds of discussions the youth minister will never be accepted by the group as someone who can at times act as leader. Moreover the lack of a negotiated agreement on what passes for acceptable behavior and what is out of order means that the youthworker may well be prevented from moving the relationship with the group on in the way that is hoped for and planned. It is a temptation to go with the energy of the young people and betray the trust of the church. This might gain some short term popularity with the group, but over the long term it will undermine the role of the youthworker as responsible adult and possibly as a herald of good news.

It is one thing to decide to be a youthworker; it can be quite another to build significant relationships with young people. Relationships bring with them spiritual responsibilities.

More often than not contact with young people can be ener-gizing and very rewarding. At times, however, it can also re-quire us to be giving in very costly ways. Extended contact is the time when young people begin to open up about what their lives are really like. We get a much clearer picture of their hopes, fears, problems, and hurts. To be a caring adult friend is a spiritual matter. It is the strength which our faith gives to us that keeps us involved when the emotional cost can be very great. Prayer sometimes becomes a matter of daily survival. We need to seek God to try make sense of what we are experi-encing as well as to gain strength.

Extended contact is also the time when our Christian identity will be explored by young people. To be involved in building relationships as an aspect of mission means that we need to be ready to offer an account of why we are doing youthwork. It is vital that we are up front and clear about who we are and what we are doing. To say that we are youth-workers attached to a church or Christian organization is gen-erally a very acceptable explanation of what we are doing. The young people we are getting to know will discover this in the natural course of a deepening relationship. There is usually little to be gained from announcing to the group on first meet-ing them that we are "Christians." They will just conclude that we are weirdos from some kind of cult. Faith is a deep and inti-mate part of our identity and one which in the normal course of things generally comes into focus quite late in relationships. Our first priority should be to meet the young people as trust-ing and trustworthy persons. Faith is integral to this for us, but the proof of the pudding is always in the eating, not the color of the label. Having said this, we must also be very clear and honest about our Christian identity when we are asked. This might simply mean that when asked what we are doing on Sunday, we say we go to church. To try to hide this in the belief that church somehow makes us unacceptable to the group is a mistake. I have had cause to learn this over again with Nick Allen, one of my colleagues from Oxford Youth Works. Each week Nick takes some record players into a local school to let a group of boys use them to mix records and rap to them. Nick regularly talks about how he uses the players and the records in church. This fact is accepted with very little if any comment by the group; it is just a fact of life when hanging out with Nick.

Nick was also the one who suggested to me that extended contact might be the time to begin to talk to young people about Jesus. He has tried on a few occasions to tell Bible stories as part of normal conversation. The idea is that the Christian youthworker follows the example of Jesus in being someone who tells stories about the kingdom. Nick says that on one occasion when he was in a pub he started to tell a Bible story to make a point in the conversation. People were leaning across the table to catch the drift of the story, such was their interest. Extended contact therefore is the time when some explicit sharing of the faith might start to take place as and when it seems appropriate. In this way the gospel message does not just appear as an agenda item further down the track without any introduction. Another way of making this kind of connection for young people is to invite them to come along to a Christian event or worship time. The purpose in this would be to give some exposure to the Christian perspective the youthworker is coming with. It is a way of starting a conversation rather than a means to a quick conversion. The likelihood is that most young people will find a church service fairly unusual and maybe a little alienating. This need not be a problem if the youth minister is able to spend time listening to what the young people are saying and offer some explanation of what was going on.

◆Proclamation

Extended contact is concerned with relationship building. During the period of extended contact we get to know a little more about the young people we are working with, and they get to know us. They will experience the care which we see as the activity of God in their lives as a sign of grace whether they know it or not. There comes a time, however, when being and doing the gospel needs to lead on to telling the story. Christian mission needs to be concerned with the Word of God proclaimed as well as with the Word of God incarnated in our lives.

It is essential that Christian youthworkers take on board the challenge of finding an appropriate way to share the gospel story with young people. Telling the story will involve allowing space for young people to question what they have heard. This testing out of the message is essential if young people are to get a handle on what the story is about and what it might mean if they were to become a part of this story. We should also allow room within our proclamation of the story for young people to make a response to the God they are hearing about and who cares for them. Proclamation therefore answers the question, "How do I share the Christian message with the young people I have come to know?"

Proclamation involves another crucial change in the dynamics of the relationship between young people and youth minister. The youthworker needs to come to terms with a movement from being an adult friend who occasionally organizes trips and events to being someone who overtly tells the gospel message. The young people for their part need to be willing to accept this change in role and allow space to hear what the youth minister is saying. This may sound very intimidating and somewhat of a daunting prospect. The key, however, will generally lie in the extent to which the youthworker has established a caring and credible presence among the group of young people. The problem is that most of us have heard horror stories, or even played our part in horror stories, where an evangelistic event has been wrecked by a group of unruly young people. An example of this would be the embarrassment of trying to conduct an altar call at the end of an open youth club. This may well be our only experience of trying to speak about Jesus to a group of unchurched young people. In most cases the young people and those doing the preaching in these situations do not know each other.

The kind of long-term relationship building which characterizes contact and extended contact means that the relationship dynamic is more established. Proclamation which follows a long-term involvement with a group of young people is therefore very different from a club epilogue. Jim Rayburn, the founder of Young Life (upon which much of this model is based), used to say that youthworkers should "Earn the right to speak."[7] By this he meant that we should have been around enough to be known and to get to know young people before we set about talking about Jesus. Preaching the gospel without relationships between the preacher and the young people may be fine when we are working Inside-Out. But in most youth

groups or churches the relational element needed for successful outreach has been provided by the friendship between
Christian young people and non-Christians. Working Outside-
In means that the youthworker must provide the relational
heart of the work.

The context in which we try to proclaim the gospel is very
important. We may well get only one chance to speak in a more
formal way about Jesus with a group of young people. If we
blow it then, it will take a good deal of work to get the group to
a point where they will accept this kind of activity again. It is
therefore very important to make clear to the young people
what we have in mind. The youth minister needs to check out
with them if it would be okay to do something which is a little
more spiritual. A discussion could be based upon a previous experience, perhaps a visit to a church or the ongoing activity of
telling stories about Jesus. In this way the idea could be presented as a question, "How would you feel about doing something like the church service we went to, but with better
music?"

My own preferred approach to proclaiming the gospel has
been to run a special camp or trip where it is clear that part of
what goes on would involve an exploration of the Christian
faith. This should be fully explained ahead of time so that the
young people can choose to sign up if they feel comfortable
with the idea. The spiritual nature of the trip should also be set
out in any publicity material used to promote the event. It is
vital that it is made clear that there is no pressure to decide to
become Christians. The main purpose of the trip would be to
inform and allow the young people to make up their own minds
on the basis of what they have heard.

The actual sharing of the gospel story needs to be thought
through in some detail. On the one hand it is crucial that the
young people are told the whole story in sufficient depth for
them to grasp what the Christian message is about. On the
other hand these will not be university theology lectures or
even church sermons. There is a need for the youthworker to
bear in mind the life experiences and social context of the
group. On the basis of this, a number of stories, primarily
about Jesus, need to be chosen which unlock the meaning of
the gospel and shed light on their normal lives. I have found a

pattern for evangelistic talks based on those used by Young Life to be very helpful:

a) Start with an experience of the young people themselves.

b) Tell a relevant story about Jesus.

c) Link the experience of the group and the Bible story.

d) Explain what this means for the young people.

e) Shut up.

This pattern is repeated over five days with the youthworker covering basic topics such as: Who was Jesus? What did he say? What did he do? Why did he die? and, How can we meet him today?

The reality is that when we move to this stage of the work, we step into the unknown with the group in a way which we have never done before. There is often a spiritual barrier which youthworkers experience when they contemplate speaking clearly about the Christian message. Sometimes this can be because of a lack of confidence in our ability to tell the gospel story. This may mean that the youthworker will need to rehearse what is to be done or get some formal training in sharing the gospel. It is also possible that the youthworker have a lack of faith that telling the message of Christ will have any effect upon a particular group of young people. This is an important spiritual challenge which needs to be overcome. There may be no substitute for just taking our life in our hands and telling the story to a group of young people. It is however possible that we can gain some confidence by recalling the power that the message about Jesus has had on us in the past or upon people we know. The gospel is a powerful message because it is rooted in God's love for us. Youthworkers need to grasp this with a confidence which can come only by continual prayer and worship.

◆Nurture

It is when young people respond to the gospel that the really demanding work starts. For youthworkers working

Outside-In, the problem of Christian nurture is not solved by an existing church-based nucleus group which can slowly socialize the young people into the faith. The most likely situation is that a small group of young people will want to explore the implications of the Christian faith in more depth. The question which relates to this stage, therefore, is, "How do we help young people learn about the faith outside of an already existing Christian group?"

The youth minister is now in a very difficult position in relation to the group. In the early stages he or she has been mainly playing the role of learner. The temptation is for the youth minister to start to play the role of the teacher, but this would be a mistake. The aim of the nurture is to see a group of young people start to explore the Christian faith themselves.[8] The end result of the stage will be a group of young people who are able to be truly Christian and yet also remain in contact with their neighborhood and their existing friendship group. We are hoping that the faith can become real within their own subcultural setting. This means that while the youthworker may know more about the details of the Christian faith, that person will not necessarily be able to make the connection between the Christian gospel and the community life of the young people.

In this situation the youth minister should act as a resource person, using experience and knowledge of the Bible and the Christian tradition to find material which might be most appropriate to the group. The role of the youthworker in this situation is primarily to act as someone who "translates" biblical stories or insights from church history and theology into the present day context of the group. This aspect of nurture and of church is explored more deeply in Chapter 5 and Chapter 7.

The youthworker tells stories and offers insights from his or her own experience and study. This material needs to be worked on by the young people to see how it makes sense for them. The most important thing is that the youthworker allows space for the young people to discuss the material and connect it with their lives. Bob Mayo says of his experience working among what he calls "pre-nonchristian young people" that he soon discovered that explaining the biblical stories was a mistake.[9] He had to be willing to tell the story from the Bible and allow the young people to make sense of it in their own terms. The key factor in this, according to Bob, is that young people from an unchurched background do not have the language to understand our explanations. The material from the Bible on the other hand is the raw stuff of revelation. The important thing is to try and make sure that our interpretation of the Bible does not get in the way of young people working it out for themselves. It is the youth minister's role to create safe places where young people can explore the Christian faith.

Nurture will generally involve some kind of group work. Young people who have decided to follow Jesus need a place where they can think in more depth about their decision. In the first instance many young people will have no idea how to pray, or how they should read the Bible, if indeed they read at all. The nurture group therefore needs to focus upon developing more than just the information about God, and the sessions should also aim to teach the right kinds of spiritual skills, e.g., methods of prayer, discussion, and worship.

Nurture should offer a chance for discussion. In some cases this will happen in a formal group and therefore needs to be facilitated in some way or another. In many cases conversations about faith will begin to permeate the activities which are more readily associated with contact work and extended contact. Nurture in this sense begins to look a little more like the kind of relationship Jesus developed among his disciples, with questions and answers, stories and explanation coming as the disciples accompanied Jesus on journeys or at meal times.

It is important to try to bridge the gap between young people and the church. As nurture starts to develop, some attempt should be made to make the young people aware of the kind of worship and fellowship that exists in local churches. It might be that full membership in a church is a little ambitious for the group. However, it is very important not to build any artificial barriers. Even more important, the youthworker needs to make clear that what happens among the young people is very much connected to the wider church.

Young Christians need constant support and help if they are to grow in the faith. The youth minister needs to build a community base where the young people can feel a sense of security without being forced into a churchy mold. This means that those involved in helping the group to explore the faith need to allow the young people to run the nurture group in a way which is most sensitive to the culture of the young people attending it. This includes the way that God is spoken about, and the prayers, worship, and social activities which surround the group must all be based within the subcultural idiom of the group.

A sensitivity to culture and to the breadth of the Christian faith requires a certain degree of theological sophistication. This kind of work is essentially a missiological task of contextualization (for more on this see Chapters 5 and 6). At a spiritual level the workers need to keep in mind that it is the Spirit of God that will lead the young people into truth. It is important to be able to operate outside of the more familiar framework which offers a greater degree of certainty in a church context. The ambiguity of trying to leave space for young people to explore the faith for themselves needs to be balanced with some idea of the limits of Christian expression and interpretation. The judgments involved in deciding what is inside the possible limits of experimentation and what is outside are far from simple. Youthworkers need to be theologically informed and spiritually sensitive.

♦Church

As Phil Moon says, the church is not an option for young Christians, it is part of the basic package.[11] This is the case whether we work Inside-Out or Outside-In. The church is the basic unit of Christian community of which we are part through our faith encounter with Christ. Our belonging to the church is first and foremost a spiritual matter. The question is how we work this out in terms of groups of people and organizations. The nucleus approach to youthwork assumes the local church as a given reality. Working Outside-In means that we have to find a solution to church for the young people we have got to know. The question for this stage is, "How can the young people who have come to faith find a place in the church?"

It may be possible for groups of young people to fit in with the life of a local congregation. However, this may not be possible or desirable. In some cases young people will want to worship in ways which reflect their own subculture, and this will be different from what happens in the church. In most cases a new worship service, separate from the adult congregation, will need to be formed to offer a church setting for the young people. This may well be linked to a local church or denominational group, but it will also need to establish a measure of independence. Either way young people who have found faith in Christ need to find a place within the broader Christian community. In some cases it will be important for the youthworker and other young adults to sign up with this community in some way. The young adults and the youthworkers can then offer a strong network within the community formed around the young people. The relationship at this point begins to move toward a more independent or interdependent contact between youthworker and young people: the youth take more responsibility for their own service, church life, fellowship, and growth. The context of the community ideally should offer a place where youthwork as such comes to an end and an ongoing life in the church context might start as the group grows more self-sufficient. This, however, may not be possible. There is some evidence that young people involved in a new worship service will eventually decide to find their own direction independent of youthworkers, however relational they may be. The role of worship and a church fellowship is therefore to provide enough experience of the faith for young people to decide in their own time what direction they will take. Youthwork should never seek to control young people, simply to offer choices. The church stage is no different in this respect.

Youthwork has as its goal the desire for young people to become independent of the youthworker. Christian youthwork will aim to offer the gospel as the context within which adult life should be lived. The move toward independence, however, may not come about without some confusion and frustration on the part of the young people and the youthworkers. If the youthworker is too directive, independence may well be delayed or may even not be achieved. This kind of dependence can be religious abuse. If on the other hand the youthworker places the responsibility of the work in the hands of the young people, the church may well descend into chaos. A balance between these two approaches is the best policy. One way of achieving this is to work with a team of helpers and the group of young people, so that the gifts needed to get the church off the ground can be found in more than one person. The problem with this, however, is that young people will still look to the youthworker they have known over a period of time for guidance and help. Relationships started through contact work and extended contact should if possible be continued into the church setting.

The main activities of the church stage will be shaped by a desire to express a corporate Christian life within the subculture of the group. In many ways the life of the group at this stage will be little different from any other church congregation. The key, however, will be to seek a new way of being church with each other. This involves imagination and creativity. These issues are examined in more depth in Chapter 7.

The church is called to be a foretaste of the kingdom of God. This means that the life of the group should be built around a desire to express in community life the values and concerns of God. Young people who have been fairly introverted within their own subculture will be challenged to open up their group life to other people. Even if it is difficult, the community will need to express its unity with other Christians in churches and congregations locally. Where a young people's expression of church is linked to one local church, this openness to other Christians is particularly important. The challenge to be a community of faith will be a struggle. The biblical picture of the church as the body of Christ, a community of priests, and a building resting on the work of Christ should offer models for the development of church life among young people.

The challenge of a Christian community is to work with the biblical demand that we are to be a holy people, set apart by God. The life of the group therefore needs to move from the acceptance of any kind of lifestyle and behavior which is common in most youth cultures to one which wrestles with the ethical demands of the gospel. To follow Christ together is to accept that he has a say in the way we live our lives. The new congregation will very soon need to work with these issues if it is to survive. The temptation is to accept everything and everyone unquestioningly. This is a mistake. On the other hand, there is the possibility that the youth minister and other church leaders may impose a set of standards upon the group which are inappropriate and insensitive. It is important to recognize that this kind of problem has been faced by the church before. When the gospel was first preached to the Gentiles, the predominantly Jewish church needed to decide if the new Christians should be expected to follow the whole of the Jewish law or some part of it. Acts 15 records how the apostles and the elders of the Jewish church, after some deliberation, came to a mind on this issue, eventually deciding that full compliance with the Jewish law was not necessary to Christian discipleship in a Gentile context. However, two laws were laid down: first, that the new Christians should refrain from eating meat which had been sacrificed to idols, and second, that they should keep a rule of chastity. Present-day Christians in working with groups of young people from subcultures so far outside of the church have a role similar to that of the Jewish church. Over time the new church will need to come to terms with difficult moral and ethical issues which arise within their own subculture. The wider church will be a resource in helping these decisions to be taken the best way possible.

Using the Model with a Nucleus Group ◆◆◆◆◆◆◆

The pattern of contact work, extended contact, proclamation, nurture, and church is really not very different for working with a church-based nucleus-fringe group. It is possible to see the nucleus group as contributing the proclamation, nurture, and church aspects of the pattern. This means that to complete the plan a church-based youthworker would need to find ways of doing contact work and extended contact as a feed into an existing group.[12]

The key to developing contact work as a means to make a nucleus group more evangelistic lies in the young people with whom the youthworker aims to work. It is a temptation for the youthworker to be drawn to the more challenging "frontier" kinds of young people. As youthworkers we often have heart for young people who are hurting or at risk. The problem with this is that if we are also committed to running youthwork in a church, we soon find ourselves operating the two disciplines at the same time. Some youthworkers are talented enough to bridge this gap, but very few of us have the time or energy to run two different patterns of ministry. Time constraints probably mean that we should look for ways of doing contact work which complement the nucleus group. This means that we should look to be making relationships with young people who we can see will eventually fit in with the existing group.

One way to build the life of the nucleus group is to develop the contact work around the young people who already come to the church group. This means setting up informal contact in schools where the Christian young people are pupils, hanging out with them at lunch times or when they are involved in activities, e.g., sports or musical interests. The aim of this will be to try to supplement the relational outreach of the nucleus group by being another Christian presence around the young people and their friends. Extended contact can then be a program of mixed activities with both Christian and non-Christian young people. The value of being involved in the lives of the Christian young people is not just evangelistic. My own experience of running a church youth group made me feel that in many ways when I was trying to teach the group from the Bible I had to guess what their lives were like. Contact work means that the youthworker has a much more acute sense of the day-to-day reality of being a Christian in school and in the other areas of teenage life.

Contact work that is done with youth who are not part of a nucleus group means that the youthworker is able to welcome fringe members into the life of the group more effectively since they already know these young people. The other advantage is that fringe members may come to one or more meetings and then drop away. Contact work offers a chance for the youthworker to informally discuss with the young person what they thought of the group and maybe find out what was going on. The dynamics of young people's lives mean that the reasons people come to groups or stop coming may have more to do with a social situation than with a spiritual decision, such as when a new visitor comes to the group because he or she is interested in one of the existing members. If the relationship doesn't work out, the newcomer may feel embarrassed to continue coming to the group. Contact work means that the youthworker is not left helpless in a sea of changing hormones. There is the chance to follow up with fringe members and try to find a way around the problems. Extended contact may also find a place in the life of nucleus group. Working with an existing friendship group of nucleus members and non-Christians, the youth minister can devise activities which build a group feel and intimacy. The important thing, however, is that these extended contact activities always build into the life of the nucleus group and do not develop a life of their own.

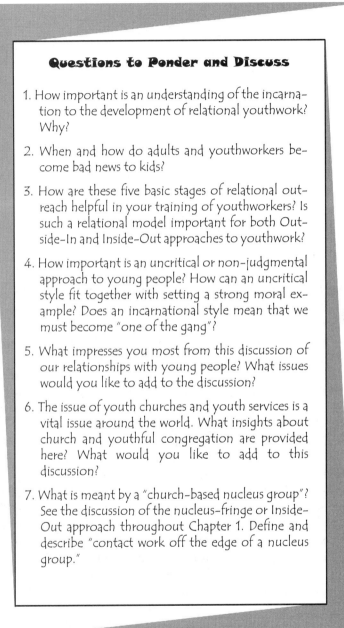

Questions to Ponder and Discuss

1. How important is an understanding of the incarnation to the development of relational youthwork? Why?

2. When and how do adults and youthworkers become bad news to kids?

3. How are these five basic stages of relational outreach helpful in your training of youthworkers? Is such a relational model important for both Outside-In and Inside-Out approaches to youthwork?

4. How important is an uncritical or non-judgmental approach to young people? How can an uncritical style fit together with setting a strong moral example? Does an incarnational style mean that we must become "one of the gang"?

5. What impresses you most from this discussion of our relationships with young people? What issues would you like to add to the discussion?

6. The issue of youth churches and youth services is a vital issue around the world. What insights about church and youthful congregation are provided here? What would you like to add to this discussion?

7. What is meant by a "church-based nucleus group"? See the discussion of the nucleus-fringe or Inside-Out approach throughout Chapter 1. Define and describe "contact work off the edge of a nucleus group."

P⊚pular Culture

An understanding of culture is basic to Christian youthwork. It is fairly obvious that the young people live and breathe their own youth cultures. Communication of any sort therefore involves some appreciation of this cultural world. Our work generally involves some understanding of concepts of popular culture and youth subcultures. Youth ministry is shaped by youth culture, but it is also shaped by the culture of the church. This means that Christian youthworkers also must be culturally bi-lingual. We understand and communicate, not only with young people, but also with churches and Christian organizations. Standing between young people on the one hand and the church on the other, we are aware that both have subcultures all of their own. The affiliation which develops around Christian music, language, and church life has much in common with the pattern of life we see among groups of young people. Thus whether working in the church, Inside-Out, or working in the community, Outside-In, the Christian youthworker needs to have developed a relatively sophisticated understanding of the issues that have to do with culture.

Current thinking concerning culture, popular culture, and subcultural theory is somewhat confused and complex. Theories of the importance and function of culture and subcultures vary. This material is important for Christian youthwork because the way we view culture will affect the way we work, both in relation to the church and in relation to young people. This chapter sets out a framework for the youthworker's encounter with culture and suggests how particular theoretical perspectives will affect the practical outworking of ministry among young people.

High Culture and Popular Culture ♦♦♦♦♦♦♦♦♦♦♦♦

The idea of culture has tended to carry with it a certain elitism.[1] It is common to regard some people as being "cultured." By this it is meant that they attend the right kind of artistic events and read the right kind of books. According to this view a visit to the opera is culture but a "Spice Girls" or "Boyzone" concert is not. Cultured people read Dickens but not Barbara Cartland. High culture is something to aspire to or improve ourselves with. Culture carries the deepest of human values, it is civilizing and spiritual. An appreciation of culture is therefore regarded as basic to education. Young people are taken on organized trips to see plays by Shakespeare or to classical concerts and art galleries. Culture is part of our heritage to be subsidized by the government and preserved for the nation in art galleries and museums.

There are certain affinities between the high culture and religion. It is possible to see the Christian faith as part of this cultural heritage. Church culture has its own contribution to make to the cultural make-up of our country. The Book of Common Prayer, The King James Version of the Bible, church music, and church architecture are themselves high culture. The church in this sense is a cultural repository, an approved and an improving experience. If we embrace an elitist view of culture, then we will expect young people to be educated into an appreciation of the cultural riches of the Christian faith as part of evangelism. Involvement in religious activity will demand considerable discipline and application on the part of young people. This kind of assumption has formed the implicit backdrop to a good deal of the church's youthwork. Through choirs, bell ringing, and serving in the liturgy many young people have been introduced both to the culture of the church and to the Christian faith. The problem is that faith as the embodiment of high culture does not especially value the culture that young people bring to the church. The expectation is that through a process of affiliation and education young people will take on the values and sensitivities of the church aesthetic and through this come to an appreciation of the spiritual values which are the reason for church music, architecture, and liturgy.

Alongside the elitist understanding of culture as high culture there has also been a tradition associated with anthropology which is more inclusive. Definitions of culture within anthropology vary, but their common characteristic tends to be a desire to include all human behavior and production. Thus culture equals: human knowledge, belief, art, morals, law, custom, economic relationships, myths and stories, sexual behavior, in fact any aspect of life which is common to members of a society. A shorthand term from the discipline of anthropology would be that culture is, "All learned human behavior."[2] Learned behavior is the cultural environment within which members of a society are born and live out their lives. Learned behavior, culture, is therefore everything which binds a society together and makes it work. The idea that different societies have different cultural frameworks and world views is a key anthropological perspective. Within the theology of mission this kind of insight has been readily adopted. Christian missionaries have long been aware that their understanding of the faith is shaped within a western cultural framework. The starting point for modern missiology therefore has generally been a desire to understand the culture of the people whom the missionaries are seeking to reach.[3]

Mission theology has developed a sophisticated understanding of the process whereby the gospel moves from one cultural framework to another. This process is described as contextualization or inculturation. These perspectives and their relevance to Christian youth ministry will be treated in more depth in the next chapter. It is important at this time to note the limitations of the anthropological view of culture for youth ministry. The overview of culture provided by anthropological definitions tends to foreshorten the tensions and cultural plurality within western societies. A macro view of culture as all things learned flattens out the subtle divisions between youth subcultures, racial groups, the impact of the media and a mass popular culture, and indeed the presence of a vibrant church subculture. Youth ministry therefore should learn from the contextualizing understanding of mission which has grown within mission studies, but it also needs to draw more deeply from current debates concerning the nature and creation of popular culture(s) within our own society.

Current understandings of popular culture have grown from a debate concerning the significance of the impact of the media and "mass culture." For early critics the media was seen as the means whereby the interests associated with business and industry manipulated the "masses" by the use of popular forms of entertainment. Popular culture was viewed with considerable suspicion because it was the means whereby capitalist interests controlled the majority of the population. Karl Marx had talked of the way that those who owned industry also controlled the means of cultural producing. This interpretation was widely accepted in the "culture industry" understanding of popular or mass culture. Religion may have declined in significance, but now it is television which has become the opiate of the masses. The emphasis upon amusement inherent within the mass media, it was argued, was there to stave off possible rebellion and social discontent. Mass culture is irretrievably imbued with the values of dominant groups in society. The masses, as they consume mass culture, are in the thrall of the values which support those with privilege. This critique of the culture industry is also essentially elitist. There are those who are in control, the elite, and there are those who are being brainwashed by television and the film industry. The brainwashed are regarded as entirely passive in the process. They are not communities or groups with a name and a life of their own. They are "the masses" at the mercy of big business and the media.

In contrast to elitist views of the culture industry or the high culture understandings of culture there has developed an appreciation of the way by which people create their own cultures. This activity has generally been referred to as "popular culture." Through the work of E. P. Thompson, Richard Hoggart, and Raymond Williams, an understanding of culture which is rooted more firmly in the everyday lives of people has been introduced.[4] Culture in this sense is no longer simply the preserve of an educated elite. In the words of Raymond Williams, "Culture is ordinary." By this he means that the language, songs, customs, games, sports, and festivities that characterize working people's lives are themselves a tradition which is filled with meaning. To understand culture in this sense is to begin to value a much broader variety of activities and cultural products as forming identity and carrying community values. Hoggart and Williams were concerned to draw a distinction between the traditional culture of the English working class and the imported "mass culture" which was being peddled by the media. "Americanization," which came with the post-war emergence of youth culture and the popularity of television and films, was seen as being a significant threat to home-grown culture. Popular culture for Williams, Thompson, and Hoggart was therefore a fairly romantic construction. As the importance of the media grew in working people's lives, the understanding and interpretation of popular culture needed to take a more positive view of "mass" culture. This perspective was provided by the growth of cultural studies.

Cultural studies were put on the map in Great Britain by the work of The Centre for Contemporary Cultural Studies (CCCS) at Birmingham University.[5] The Centre was originally set up by Richard Hoggart, but his work was taken further by Stuart Hall, who along with a number of others set about a program of studying the meanings behind aspects of popular culture. Central to this project was primarily the study of television and then youth culture. The study of youth culture therefore provides a useful introduction to the main findings of cultural studies.

Subculture ◆◆◆◆◆◆◆◆◆◆◆◆◆◆◆◆◆◆◆◆◆◆◆◆◆◆◆◆◆◆◆

Anthropological insights tend to treat culture as a single unified system of meaning. The conception of subculture, however, is based upon the realization that "learned behavior" depends upon the context within which that learning takes place.

Societies are divided by a number of inequalities. Traditionally sociology has described these inequalities in terms of race, gender, and social class. These "strata" give shape to the variety of opportunity and community identity which individuals experience in life. Who we are is fundamentally shaped by the community within which we learn behavior. We make sense of our identity and our place in the larger societal system on the basis of our location in the various strata.[6] Thus a young Asian woman growing up in a poor, urban community may well inhabit a very different subcultural world from a that of a young white man growing up in the leafy suburbs of an upper-class neighborhood.

For Stuart Hall and those in the CCCS, the concept of subculture was used to explain the existence of "resistant cultures" within society. Drawing on the work of the Italian theorist Gramsci, Hall argued that culture provided an arena within which different groups in society carried out a struggle. Those groups which are economically and socially dominant seek to extend their authority by using culture to support their power. Culture then becomes a means for dominant groups in society to seek the assent of subordinate groups. When this assent is achieved it is called "hegemony" by Gramsci. At the same time subordinate groups use the cultural arena as a means to create pockets of resistance. Hall combined these insights from Gramsci concerning culture as an arena for struggle with the theories concerning culture as a series of signs and symbols which was developed by the French philosopher Roland Barthes. Hall's understanding of youth culture was that it was an attempt to resist "hegemony" by creating subcultures. These subcultures are created by the use of particular kinds of dress, ways of behaving, and ways of speaking which are laden with symbols and signs. The analysis of signs and symbols found in Barthes was used as the means to understand the meaning of youth subcultures such as "Punk" or "Mod." The symbols when correctly understood reveal a style of life which is an attempt to create identity apart from that offered by the dominant culture; it is therefore "resistant."[7]

At the CCCS various youth subcultures in England were seen as the cultural products of mainly blue-collar young people. In the book *Resistance through Rituals,* the style of punks, skinheads, and other teenage groups in England are said to reveal symbolic meanings that point to "contradictions" in society. In the case of skinheads, the contradiction experienced was seen as the erosion of traditional blue-collar communities. The widespread growth in unemployment was aggravated by the recent influx of Asian people newly arrived from India, Pakistan, and Bangladesh. The response of blue-collar young people was to create a distinctive style that included Doc Martins, suspenders, and a shaven head. This style was seen by the authors of *Resistance through Rituals* as signifying a desire to return to the pure blue-collar roots. Through developing distinctive ways of dress, music, and behavior, young people are able to make "cultural space" for themselves. In this cultural space they find meaning and identity over and against the dominant culture. Although the dominant culture might view them as hooligans and thugs, the young skinhead will see himself as "cool" and "hard." To be cool and hard is to assert the right to an identity which is achieved through membership in the informal subcultural group rather than through conformity to the wider society.

The key interpretative framework used to understand youth subculture in *Resistance through Rituals* was social class. Youth culture was seen as the means whereby blue-collar young people who were seen as being economically, educationally, and socially disadvantaged achieved a sense of identity and therefore resistance. However, *Resistance through Rituals* was criticized for reading youth subculture based exclusively upon social class, most notably by Angela McRobbie. McRobbie argued that the reading of youth subcultures adopted by Hall and others tended to focus upon young men. The place of subculture within the lives of young women remained largely hidden. McRobbie has developed this insight, and in her later books *Gender and Generation* and *Feminism and Youth Culture* she has sought to shed light upon the way that women use shopping as means to create identity and meaning. Rather than being expressed in terms of the hegemonic struggle between social classes, McRobbie's understanding of popular culture has been framed by a feminist understanding of a society that is shaped by male patriarchy. Young women, she argues, are faced with a need to negotiate their sense of identity and worth in relation to the dominant view of women which is presented in advertising, TV shows, and teenage girls' magazines.

Michael Brake extended the study of youth culture by studying not only blue-collar groups but also middle-class ones. He points out how the middle classes in Great Britain have had a tradition of bohemian artistic lifestyles, which have developed subcultures that are themselves "counter cultural" and resistant to the dominant culture. An example would be the 1960's hippie movement, which was almost exclusively middle-class in origin. Whether blue-collar or middle-class, Brake points out, the attempt to create subcultures by young people is usually temporary and unsuccessful. The reason for this is that the "contradictions" in society that have given rise to the creation of the subculture are resolved only at a cultural level. The initial sparking point in the creation of a subculture, he argues, will generally be economic, e.g., the fact that many black young people experience disadvantage in getting jobs. Looking good and having the right haircut may bring a measure of self-respect and group identity, but it does not solve the real problem of the lack of adequate or suitable employment.

The meaning of subcultural style may be more than the creation of group identity. Dick Hebdige, writing as punk began to appear on the streets of Great Britain, saw style as a means to generate shock. Young people, according to Hebdige, form new subcultures by the creative bringing together of symbolic ways of dressing. Hebdige uses the term "bricolage" to describe the chaotic combination of items of dress. The new combination carries with it the associations and meanings of each of the items of dress. By bringing together disparate items group members disassociate these new meanings from their original context and relocate them within a new identity. Thus in punk, bondage gear that was usually associated with sexual fetish and hidden in the private world of sado-masochism was used as an everyday fashion item. This was combined with mohawk hair cuts and tartan kilts. Subcultural style thus became a means to disturb and create questions, contradicting the usual role of dress, which is to reassure and locate individuals and groups within an understood social structure. Style is therefore a means to wage war on the public by the use of disturbing combinations of symbols and signs.

Hebdige identified the crucial role played by those who were in the vanguard of the creation of particular subcultural styles. It is in these groups, where a style first emerges, argues Hebdige, that the cultural analyst is to look for meaning. Crucial to the original creation of subcultures and styles is the way that white young people interact with subcultures that have emerged within black communities, particularly in the United States. An example of this would be the way that suburban white young people have in more recent times adopted the music, dress, and street language associated with rap and hip hop, which originally comes out of the urban African-American context. The spread of subcultural style, however, according to Hebdige, represents a slow disintegration of meaning as aspects of the subculture are picked up by mainstream fashion. Thus an item of clothing first made by art school students or worn by trend-setting musicians is soon copied by the fashion industry and marketed to young people all around the country. The fashion business and the commercial interests of the shops tend to modify the subcultural look, softening it, with the result that the manufactured version of a subcultural style has generally lost much of its original shock value. This process of adoption brings a gentler, less challenging edge to the style, making it more acceptable and less meaningful. Hebdige's early understanding of youth culture is therefore somewhat elitist. The trend setters are the true source of meaning. As the style spreads it becomes diluted and corrupted. Hebdige therefore sees the consuming of the average young person as lacking the real cutting edge of cultural criticism and creative energy that is seen in the art-school world of the avant garde. His work is to be seen in contrast to the work of people like McRobbie who have emphasized the creative act that young women in particular engage in as they shop. For her, cultural creativity and meaning is open to all young people.

For subcultural theorists, style has always been wider than how young people dress. In *Resistance through Rituals* Paul Corrigan described the behavior of a group of young people in an essay called "Doing Nothing."[8] Corrigan investigated how groups of young people hanging around on the streets organized their time. His work uncovered the way that the group would gather in the same place waiting for something to happen. This behavior was often mundane, but it held within it the possibility of excitement. Excitement might come when someone decided to kick a beer bottle around or when someone got hold of a moped and drove around the neighborhood in an entertaining manner. Gangs of young people on the streets may appear unoccupied and somewhat threatening to the wider community, but Corrigan shows how a community relationship and activity are sustained for many young people when they are "doing nothing." A complementary picture of young people's lives is shown by Marsh, Rosser, and Harre, who studied the behavior of groups of soccer supporters at Oxford United's playing field. The record of these studies, *The Rules of Disorder,* shows how the crowd is organized with different positions within the Oxford Rd. End (the part of the stadium where Oxford United's fans stand).[9] The authors were able to observe by examining videotape taken over a whole year that particular people stood in the same places in the stand every week. Some were younger boys on the fringe of things, others were "the guys," others were older people who had once been where the action was, and others were the cheer leaders who started the chants going. These positions in the stand indicated a definite hierarchy and career pattern for the football supporter. What might be seen as "mob" behavior tinged with anarchy, according to *The Rules of Disorder,* is actually a well-organized social system based on commonly understood rules of behavior. For those at the center of "disorder" there is actually order and community.

The British tradition of cultural studies represented by writers such as Hall, Brake, Hebdige, and McRobbie has tended to locate meaning in popular culture within a struggle for identity between dominant culture and subcultures. This struggle might be variously understood as being based on social class, gender, or race; however, the key dynamic remains the same. Young people create a sense of self, community life, and meaning by symbolic consumption and behavior. They do this by the creative use of cultural artifacts delivered to them by the widespread availability of the products of mass production. The relationship between the industry of popular culture and the young people who consume the products of this industry forms the basis for the continuing discussion of popular culture.

Slaves to the Rhythm ◆◆◆◆◆◆◆◆◆◆◆◆◆◆◆◆◆◆◆◆◆◆

The rise of popular culture has been seen by many Christians as a far-from-positive development. When dealing with youth culture and the role of the media, a somewhat uniform Christian version of the argument against the culture industry has generally been adopted. According to this view, the media carries within it a "materialistic" message that is against the Christian gospel. The influence of advertising, television, and pop music upon young people is viewed as a "bad thing." Popular music encourages hedonism, sexual promiscuity, idolatry, and the occult. Christian young people should be warned of the dangers of listening to the wrong kind of music or watching the wrong kind of shows. According to the authors of *Dancing in the Dark,* modern media has found ways to market its products to what they call "generational groups."[10] The identification of separate age-related "markets" for consumer products has meant that youth culture has been shaped by powerful economic forces. The culture industry has therefore created "youth culture" to provide a willing and accessible group to whom products can be sold. The generation gap is a reality, but it is by no means an insurmountable problem, argues *Dancing in the Dark.* Indeed, conflict between the young and the old is not a new phenomenon; it is evident in ancient Greek and biblical periods. What is new is that advertising and industry have in recent times sought to exploit these conflicts to sell into a designated and committed market. In this way separation between generations has been exaggerated to serve the ends of industry and multi-national corporations. Young people, according to this view, are therefore manipulated and duped by an all-powerful media that holds all the cards.

The manipulative view of popular culture prevalent within Christian circles (especially in the US) owes a good deal to the work of Neil Postman. Postman argues that technologies of communication have an impact upon the way that we discuss the world.[11] Thus, the arrival of the telegraph in the US brought about the culture of the news. The invention of the telegraph meant that communications between towns and countries became much quicker than the pace of a letter carried by horse or train. Suddenly it was possible to receive reports of events around the world almost instantaneously, and the news as we know it was born. But the telegraph not only increased the pace by which "news" could be spread, it also packaged that news into short segments. The technology needed relatively short sentences and paragraphs that could be sent down the wires quickly and received with the minimum of misunderstanding. The news spoke of events from all over the country and eventually the world, but the seeming expansion of vision also brought a contraction of perspective. This contraction is imposed upon reality by the nature of the media used to convey the message. The selection and packaging of material to be sent as news inevitably affects the way that the world is viewed. A similar packaging can be seen as a result of the development of radio and television.

The process of cultural change led by technologies of communication has been a steady process of erosion. According to Postman, television brings with it a reduction of rational discussion. On television the sound bite has made political discussion into a short advertisement. How a politician looks is more important than what he or she says. The "sound bite" is more important than extended conversation on political matters. Image has triumphed over content, and the reason for this is that television has become the chief arena for political discourse. The nature of the medium, argues Postman, is that it processes everything that it treats and homogenizes it into entertainment. In this way the distinctions between fact and fantasy are blurred. On television the assassination of a world leader, the latest video from a pop group, and a soap opera, all seemed to look the same. Real life tragedy and fictional disaster and technicolor advertising are all offered for our amusement. Entertainment—not truth—is the primary logic of television.

These kinds of insights have been seized on by Christians as evidence of moral corrosion associated with the media and popular culture. The role of Christian youthwork is to help young people to "critique" what is presented to them by the media. According to John Buckeridge, Christians are to be particularly wary of advertising.[12] The millions spent by multinationals on researching youth culture is seen as good reason to warn young people that subtle and well-financed organizations are attempting to "control" them. An all-out conspiracy theory is only just avoided, but all the same "youth culture" is viewed as being an arena that is full of dangers. This is well-illustrated by the way that some youth ministry magazines run stories that tell of the "occult" leanings of particular records or stars, or give alarming statistics of the use of drugs or the attitudes of pop singers.[13]

Inherent to these kinds of attitudes toward the media is the view that young people are at risk and "impressionable." In contrast to the secular tradition of cultural studies, Christians have rarely attempted to value the culture that young people themselves create. Youth culture is more often seen in terms of a particular reading of the products that are offered to young people by the culture industry. Thus the media is regarded as powerful and dangerous. Young people themselves are seen as in need of instruction or even protection from the influence of advertising and youth culture. This kind of motivation can be seen in Christian campaigns against sexually explicit or violent videos or records. At the same time Christians have been very keen to develop their own alternative subculture for young people. This subculture has been created and maintained by Christian youthworkers.

Evangelical Christians have tended to be proactive in their use of modern technology and media to spread the gospel. Printing, radio, television, video, satellite, cable, the internet—whatever new developments have come along have been used by Christians for "the kingdom." Youthworkers have been right at the heart of these innovations. Youth ministry has been the means whereby the cultural forms associated with youth culture have been "Christianized." Thus we get Christian rap music and Christian dance music, etc. The intention behind these developments has been the creation of alternative Christian subcultures for young people. Through festivals, concerts, tapes, and CDs, young people are invited to consume the products of the Christian media industry. The problem with this approach is that it is still informed by an elitist "culture industry" understanding of popular culture. Youth ministry has tended to focus attention on the content of the products of Christian media rather than on how young people use these products to create identity.

Christian commentators have generally adopted a negative view of popular culture. In some of the material developed within cultural studies, a more positive view of meaning-making and creativity-from-below has developed. A theological understanding of the Christian subculture will therefore need to focus not simply on the content and message of particular texts produced by Christian artists, it will also have to ask questions of how these texts are given meaning and significance by young people themselves. The key to this will be the development of a more sophisticated understanding of the relationship between cultural texts and the subcultures which young people create.

Identity and Popular Culture ◆◆◆◆◆◆◆◆◆◆◆◆◆◆◆

In *Common Culture,* Paul Willis examines the artistic life of young people. In contrast to art with a capital "A," young people's lives, argues Willis, are to be seen as creative and imaginative. While most young people may well not be involved in the arts, their everyday lives are full of expressions, signs, and symbols. These are used by individuals and groups to establish their "presence" in society. The popular aesthetic of young people is used to build identity and meaning. This creative aspect of youth culture can be seen in the clothes that young people wear, in the way they do their hair, in the pictures they use to decorate their bedrooms, in their use of slang, in the piercing and tattooing of their bodies, in the dances they create, and in the drama and ritual in their relationships.[14] Willis uses the concept of "necessary work" to describe the importance of these symbolic modes of communication and association. Necessary work is that which we need to do in order to survive. For young people, passing through adolescence means that they are in one way or another marginalized. The establishment of a sense of who they are in relation to others, says Willis, is a matter of survival and therefore necessary.[15]

Willis' view of youth culture is complemented by the work of John Fiske. Fiske argues that as long as the culture industry fills its products with meanings, these meanings will always need to find a resonance in people's lives.[16] The fact that many big-budget movies often fail at the box office is an indication that, despite its advertising and promotional power, the media is not as able to manipulate young people as some critics and Christians suggest. Similarly, in the record business the vast numbers of singles which are released each month in the UK should cause some pause for thought. Of the 700 or so released every week, only a very small proportion ever find success. This means that the music industry is largely at the mercy of the buying public. Popular culture therefore, for Fiske, resides in the way that groups of people create their own meanings from the products they are offered. Mass culture that is manufactured and passed down to young people and others is largely a myth. Culture is a living thing that can be developed only from within; it cannot be imposed from above. The culture industry produces a repertoire of texts that groups of people use to create their own popular cultures.[17]

Willis uses the term common culture for the process described by Fiske. Common culture refers to the necessary symbolic work of young people. Modern societies, according to Willis, are ones where traditional sources of meaning, belonging, and security have been eroded. The conception of a "whole" culture with defined places of meaning and understood roles and identities has long since passed. Organized religion, political affiliation, an identity supplied by location in the workplace, schools, and public broadcasting no longer offer commonly held values. In the past the passage from childhood to adulthood was well-defined and structured. This passage has become more complicated and consequently less easy to traverse. For young people marginalized from publicly understood sources of meaning, things such as the certainties of previous generations and existing institutions—which they see as merely living off the capital of the past—no longer remain plausible.[18] For those who might be seen as being on the edge of society, teenagers or minorities, these problems are particularly acute. The response has been the establishment of common cultures rooted in what Willis calls a "grounded aesthetic," i.e., a sense that what is culturally acceptable comes from young people themselves rather than from an artistic or indeed a religious establishment.[19] Common culture is seen in the way that young people and young adults are able to create "proto-communities."[20] These are informal communities that form around particular interests or events. Individuals may from time to time find themselves involved in a number of proto-communities. Proto-communities locate around a shared sense of style, a set of behaviors, or an issue-based political group. An example of the latter might be animal rights activists, or "save the environment" groups, in which the community of people that is brought together transcends the divisions usually associated with race, gender, or social class. These kinds of "proto-communities" offer an impermanent sense of identity and purpose.

The Limitations of Cultural Studies ♦♦♦♦♦♦♦♦♦

The work of people like Fiske and Willis has encountered criticism from within the discipline of cultural studies. Jim McGuigan argues that what has emerged in recent times is an uncritical acceptance that significant meaning resides with the cultures created by groups of people. He calls this view "cultural populism" in that it simply describes and celebrates popular culture.[21] The sense that cultural texts such as television might be read and critiqued in a literary manner has largely been abandoned by many within cultural studies in the face of the meanings which people make from television, says McGuigan. The meaning of soap opera, for instance, has been presented as the way it offers particular "pleasures" which derive from the way that the individual viewer reads the text, rather than the meaning which is located in the program by industry or the script writer. Any confidence in a critical judgment as to the value or appropriateness of a particular cultural text has therefore tended to be left on one side. This lack of a critical perspective is largely the result of the collapse of a shared framework within which to assess the cultural value of texts. The confidence in a critique of culture has tended to be linked to the acceptance of an overarching theory, e.g., high culture or the hegemonic struggle of different groups or the feminist interpretation of patriarchal structures of society.

For Christians engaged in working with young people, the insights and the limitations of cultural studies are particularly informative. In the first place, the work of people such as Hall or McRobbie indicates that as young people construct identities, they may well be doing so in reaction to problems of an economic or social nature. The Christian youthworker will want to first understand the signs and symbols of young people's style, because these offer an insight into the social issues that concern groups of young people. If the gospel is to be good news for young people, then it must be seen to encounter social as well as personal issues. The subculture created by young people therefore becomes the means by which the gospel can become meaningful within a particular subculture. This contextualizing will seek to express the faith within the language and style of the group, but it will also at the same time develop a sensitivity to the underlying "contradictions" from which the subculture has emerged.

For this reason, it is unrealistic to try to create a Christian subculture that is a safe retreat from the rest of the world. To offer an alternative subculture to that which young people themselves have constructed is to miss the indications of how the gospel might be of more long-term relevance within communities. Youth culture indicates the areas where the power of God might start to be at work to bring about social change and transformation. Youth culture has highlighted issues concerning the environment and has led protests against war. It is in relation to these kinds of issues that Christian youthworkers can learn a good deal from the work of people such as Willis and Fiske. At the same time cultural studies indicate that Christian young people are vital to the creation of a specifically Christian subculture within the church. The assumption that Christian music is good and safe needs to be examined in the light of the work of cultural theorists such as Willis. Cultural studies point us away from the cultural texts—such as TV, film, and music—and toward the culture which Christian young people themselves create. Our understanding of how the Christian subculture actually operates is at the present time fairly limited. We all swim in the pool, but we have never really analyzed the water.

Cultural studies may well have lost a shared framework for critiquing culture, but Christians have not. The basis for our engagement in communities will remain the gospel. Andrew Walker refers to this as the "grand narrative" of the Christian church.[22] It is this narrative (summarized in Chapter 2) that gives us a critical perspective on popular culture. It draws cultural analysis into a new framework of gospel truth. This is both affirming and negative. However, this is somewhat different from the usual Christian approach to popular culture. Christian cultural analysis has tended to concentrate on youth culture as either a threat or as competition to the subculture offered by the church. The rise of the Christian subculture has been generated by the feeling that a safe religious alternative to the harmful influence of popular youth culture should be offered to young people. The net result has been that the church has regarded indigenous youth subcultures as "competition." Youth ministry has used the same methods as those which exist in the secular scene. Christian festivals compete in the same market place as non-Christian festivals. Christian bands sell their products to young people in the same way as non-Christian artists. They each compete financially for young people's money, and they compete for loyalty. Christian youth groups often feel that they are working in competition against the draw of sporting activities or other entertainments. Many youth ministers feel a sense of helplessness in the face of the increasing attractiveness of the popular media. There is also the possibility that those in the church feel a sense of threat when young people adopt particular styles of dress. These attitudes come about not so much because of the demands of the gospel but because of the mindset which arises from the attempt to compete in the marketplace with popular culture. To engage missiologically with a culture is somewhat different from attempting to establish a substitute culture that young people can buy into. The discipline of seeking to see the good news come alive within popular culture has a different trajectory than trying to tempt young people away from the culture that they themselves have adopted and created.

In the light of the gospel story, Christian youthworkers will be looking for those aspects of popular culture that they can see as being in tune with the gospel, while at the same time working for renewal and transformation of those aspects that are outside the sweep of God's intentions for society. Cultural studies therefore give us tools to understand the culture of groups of young people, but it is the gospel that gives us a perspective to see these in a fresh light.

Questions to Ponder and Discuss

1. Do you agree that "an understanding of culture is basic to Christian youthwork"? Have you seen a sensitivity to and awareness of culture reflected in the teaching and materials available to most youth ministers? Are you aware of new studies on culture, subcultures, and pop culture?

2. Do you agree that "The church . . . is a cultural repository." What do you see as the relationship between culture and religion? Central to our evaluation of youth churches must be an understanding of worship, high culture, and low culture. Do you see the possibility of cultural problems when you bring young people into the church?

3. What is meant by youthful "resistance through rituals"?[23]

4. Do we in youth ministry need to be cultural critics? Do we need to see the positive aspects of all cultures and subcultures before we, with the help of those within the culture, look at its negative aspects? Do you see the positive in current (extremes of) youthful fashions, music, and entertainment?

5. How do the young people you want to reach create meaning and clarify their own personal identities within their friendship groups?

Youthwork and the Incarnation of the Word

There is no technique or method that guarantees results for the Christian youthworker. However skilled and experienced we may be, at the heart of our work is a mystery. This mystery is based on the spiritual nature of what we are doing. What makes Christian youthwork distinctive is the belief that through our practice Jesus wishes to become real in young people's lives. The presence of Jesus can be expressed in terms of "incarnation," i.e., God taking flesh. Christian youthwork is therefore a combination of our knowledge, skill, and practice, and God's energy.

God's presence in our work and in the lives of the young people we are meeting is not a right, it is a blessing. We cannot expect that through our actions God will be present; neither can we assume that a professional incompetence or lack of skill as a youthworker might mean that God is not present. The mystery of Christian youthwork is that "the wind blows where it wills." We have no idea how the Holy Spirit is moving in the lives of the young people. The mission is God's. We are joining in with God's activity, not God with ours. In mission God is sovereign. To forget this is to make of our practice an idol. God becomes controlled by our programs and expectations and thus no God at all.

The "spiritual" nature of Christian youthwork is not to be expressed at the expense of human knowledge, expertise, and skill. To reach out with the gospel means that we must be able to communicate effectively within the cultural world of the young people we are meeting. The importance of the work of God and our own efforts is expressed in an "incarnational" theology of mission. This chapter examines the human side of mission among young people.

An incarnational theology of mission involves three kinds of journeys, each of which requires particular skill and expertise. The first is the generational journey that all adults need to make in order to communicate with young people. The youthworker needs to be willing and able to step outside the "adult" way of relating and find a way to make contact within the natural environment of the teenager. The second journey involves a movement from one social subgroup to another. The youthworker needs to be able to understand and communicate within the language patterns, social system, and symbolic frameworks of a particular group. Some youthworkers may have grown up in the same sort of setting as that in which they are ministering, enabling them to communicate "naturally." However, the majority must journey past a cultural barrier to the social place where their young people live. The third journey is from a place of faith to a place of no faith. The first two journeys all youthworkers have in common, the third is unique to Christian youthwork. This chapter provides a basic framework to enable Christian youthworkers to understand how the faith becomes "incarnated in culture."

Aspects of the Incarnation of the Word in Culture ◆◆◆◆◆◆◆◆◆◆◆◆◆◆◆◆◆◆◆◆◆◆◆◆◆◆◆◆◆◆◆◆◆

◆The Incarnation of Jesus

The Christian faith rests on the belief that God became human in Jesus Christ. Jesus is "The Word" become flesh, God's revelation within human history and human culture.

When God chooses to communicate, God uses the language, customs, and social relationships of a particular group of people in a particular time and in a particular place. Jesus was therefore a Jew born into a Jewish family. This means that the content of the "good news" as we see it in the gospels is intimately connected to the social, political, and spiritual context within which Jesus grew up and began to minister. This location of the Word of God within culture must be taken seriously by any Christian seeking guidance from the life of Christ. For while we may want to assert that God is revealed in the life of Jesus, we must also acknowledge that this life was lived out in a time that was quite different from our own. The fact that the word of God was incarnated within a human culture brings God closer to us, but it also creates a cultural distance for us.

Understanding the gospel story involves a process of thinking ourselves into the social world of the New Testament. We cannot read the gospels directly into our present-day experience. The setting of the story colors not only the message of Christ but also the way that good news takes shape in people's lives. The incarnation of Jesus forces the reader to deal with another culture and another time as the "medium" within which eternal truth is played out. Thus the cultural setting of the life of Christ forms an irreducible aspect of the story. This does not mean that we cannot understand the gospel or interpret it for today, nor does it mean that we have to be biblical scholars to get any kind of message from the text of Scripture. It simply means that we have to work with the gospel text as a narrative that is located in a particular historical time.

The life of Christ is the revelation of God within culture. The location of the incarnation within a defined cultural setting means that we have no knowledge of God outside of culture. To meet God through the story of Jesus in the New Testament is an experience within the culture, religious history, and tradition of the Jews. God uses this culture to become known. A careful interpretation involves the reader in first considering the setting in life of the passage that is under consideration. This means the particular social and cultural situation of the passage, but it also means viewing the passage in the light of a reading of the whole of the New Testament and the Old Testament. This kind of interpretative process arises directly from the means by which God has chosen self-revelation.

The Christian faith in the present era (or indeed at any time) is always an interpretation of the message. In each age the church has the task of reading the Bible and making sense of it within its own social and cultural setting. The gospel that we have received and that has possibly changed our lives is still only one possible "contextualization" of the faith within culture. Culture is the medium within which faith is expressed and lived out. This insight does not mean that what we have received as the truth is in some way wrong. It simply means that we need to acknowledge the provisional nature of the faith as we understand it. The church believes that it is the Holy Spirit who leads us into truth. It is the Spirit working within the body of believers who makes it possible to embrace our cultural expressions of the gospel as "truth." When Christians express the message of the gospel, we do so within our own cultural frameworks.

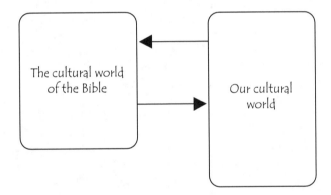

The Christian faith must be expressed within culture for it to come alive for people. It is the task of the church and of individual Christians to proclaim the message of Christ. Our proclamation, however, is not authoritative in itself. It is the revelation of Christ in the Bible which remains our sole authority. While we must seek to speak of God within our culture, our confidence in our own expression of the faith must be regarded as only one possible expression of the faith. When our theological deductions from the scriptures become confused with scripture itself, we become idolatrous, i.e., we have substituted our words for the word of God. Such idolatry is particularly prevalent where the church is so identified with one particular culture that it has become culturally blind. It is the experience of Christians within other cultural contexts that alerts us to this kind of blindness. When we hear the Word of God expressed within another set of cultural norms, we suddenly become aware of our own cultural conditioning.

For the youthworker an understanding of the cultural nature of the Christian faith is fundamental. Self-awareness is the basis for mission across cultures. The first step to accomplishing that mission among young people from outside of the subculture of the church is an understanding of our own subcultural makeup. One way to achieve this is to spend time with Christians from other parts of the world. The experience of faith contextualized in other cultures helps us to relativize our own understanding of the faith. This sets us free to imagine the gospel expressed in new ways. In *Youth Culture and the Gospel,* I set out to express this by showing a number of pictures of Jesus drawn by Christians from around the world.[1] The African picture showed a black Jesus, the Japanese picture showed Jesus as an oriental, and of course the Western Jesus was a white man. These different pictures give a clue as to the way that faith can be expressed within culture. They also point to our cultural bondage. This is particularly the case where we find it hard to accept a picture of Jesus which is different from our own. The youth minister working across cultures and subcultures will need to develop an awareness of the way that his or her own understanding of the Christian faith has been shaped within a particular culture. This self-awareness is the first step in contextualizing the gospel.

◆*Incarnation = Being With*

All youthwork is based on relationships with young people. Christian youthwork is no different except that we see relationships not just as an end in themselves but as the means by which young people may experience the presence of Christ. The Christian youthworker is seeking to be a concrete expression of the Christian faith among a group of young people. "Being with" young people and getting involved in their lives expresses this incarnational truth. There are Christian approaches to youthwork that do not rely upon relationship. An example would be the evangelist who arrives for a mission at a school one week and next week moves on to the next. This pattern of youthwork may have its place, but it is not incarnational, in that it lays very little, if any, emphasis upon the ongoing presence of the youthworker with a group of young people.

Incarnational youthwork as a method of outreach has much in common with the work of Christian missionaries. Missionaries such as Bible translators have evolved a long-term plan for the way that the gospel should be shared with groups of people who have not heard the message. The Bible translator will prepare by developing a full acquaintance with the Bible in its original languages. Academic study of the Bible is necessary because the task is to translate the text from the original languages into the thought forms and language of the new group of people. This preparation, which takes a long time and much study, is only half of what is required. Having studied the Bible, the translator must then get to know the culture of the people with whom he or she wishes to share the message. This means going and living with the people over a long period of time so that the structure, grammar, and vocabulary of the language can be learned. The effective translator will need to understand the ritual and symbolic language of the community, and there is no shortcut to this. The translator must be so involved in the life of the people as to develop a true understanding of the community through observation and through conversations with the people. In some situations the translator has had to create a written form of a language that has so far only ever been spoken. This is necessary before it is possible to translate the biblical text into that language. When it comes to translating, the missionary will ideally not be seeking a literal expression of the biblical text, because the message will need to be contextualized. This is done by what Charles Kraft calls dynamic equivalents in translation, e.g., in communities where sheep do not exist, other animals might be used to translate the image of Jesus as the Lamb of God.[2] By these kinds of means a presentation of the biblical message can emerge which is true to the original text, but which also makes sense in the culture of the people.

For Christian youthwork "being with" must precede any verbal expression of the faith. Like the translator of the Bible, the youth minister is also in a missionary situation of moving from one cultural setting to another. After first learning the Bible, we must learn the language, social behavior, values, and symbolic expressions of the young people we are working with. The only way that we can do this is to spend time in regular informal contact with the young people we want to reach. Informal time means that we are not running a program or a meeting. It means that we are in contact with the group when they are relating naturally. When we are in charge of a meeting, young people tend to conform to our ways of speaking and relating. When we are doing contact work with them, they relate in ways which are more indigenous to them. It is only when we are "being with" a group as they relate normally that we are able to understand and communicate within their particular subculture.

The time we spend in informal contact with young people forms the basic resource for our verbal proclamation of the gospel. If we cut short informal time, or if we dispense with it altogether, we have no guarantee that what we are doing is a contextualization of the faith. The likelihood is that as we share the faith we impose our own culture at the same time. We are resorting to the same sort of cultural imperialism as did the missionaries who exported the English Victorian, Gothic church architecture, music, and worship to Africa and India. Being with young people gives us the ability to see the gospel through their eyes, so that when we come to "translate" the message for them, we do so out of a respect for and intimacy with their own subculture and social context.

Being with, however, is itself an expression of the gospel. As we spend time with young people, we find that we are a reflection of the love of God among them. The respect we show as we spend time getting to know groups and individuals is a witness to the presence of Christ among the group. The way we go about outreach among young people is therefore a sign of the gospel. We are the means by which Jesus becomes incarnated among a group of young people. To be "incarnational" as a youthworker is therefore to live out a spirituality that is deeply rooted in the life of Christ. We are imitators of Christ attempting, by the things we do and say, to offer young people an insight into the heart God has for them. Our concern is a powerful sign of God's regard for young people. The things that we disapprove of similarly indicate the priorities of the kingdom of God. An incarnational approach to youthwork would hold that the way we share the gospel is as much a sign of the good news as what we say. By implication it would distance itself from methods of evangelism that seem to violate this principle.

◆The Word in Translation

Translation of the gospel rotates around three poles: the Bible, the culture of the translator, and the culture of the people for whom the translation is being made.

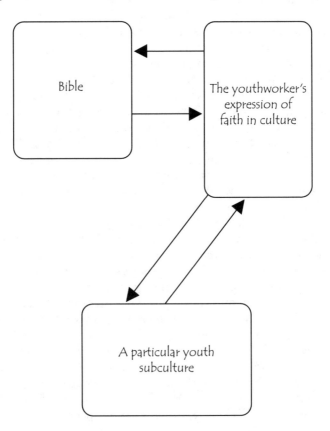

Bible

The youthworker's expression of faith in culture

A particular youth subculture

Sharing the faith from one culture to another or from one subculture to another is based upon the interaction of these three poles. First the youthworker needs to have a good grasp of the biblical material. This is a part of youthwork training that can sometimes be missed. In particular we can be guilty of a favorite passage or proof-text approach to reading the scriptures. Youthworkers are often activists and reluctant to spend long periods of time reading material that does not immediately affect our work, even if what we are reading is the Bible. Being with young people often feels more attractive than academic study. The current enthusiasm for worship can also erode our familiarity with the Bible. For some youthworkers brought up on charismatic worship, a commitment to the study of the Bible can seem a little tame. These tendencies have weakened our ability to translate the message to young people who are outside of the social groups that currently make up the church.

We need to read the whole of the Bible to have firm grasp on the gospel story. If we keep to well-trodden paths or rely upon the immediacy of the Spirit in worship, our problem is that we have not allowed the Bible to call our assumptions about the faith into question. Karl Barth entitled one of his early essays "The Strange New World Within the Bible."[3] The youthworker needs to spend time exploring the depth and variety of the strange new world of the Bible. Regular in-depth Bible study that takes us into the less well-known parts of the text introduces us to people whose experience of God was very different from our own. In the strange new world of the Bible we find that the nice caring "Father" of our choruses and church worship seems to engage in a good deal of judgment and bloodshed. Moreover, in the Bible we discover that people whom we would never put into leadership in our groups seem to be used by God to bring about heavenly purposes. When we move away from the familiar territory of scripture into less well-known paths, we are surprised by the sheer variety of ways of talking about God, praying, and worshiping that we find expressed in the Bible.

Entering the strange new world of the Bible gives us a clue that the Christian faith as we have been taught it is conditioned by culture. The rich diversity of spiritual experience and expression in the biblical material gives us an indication that our own practice, though very helpful and relevant, may not be the only possible way of living out the Christian faith. This sense of "relativity" concerning the tradition which we have inherited is essential to successful translation. Without the possibility that the Christian faith might look and sound different, the translator will tend to replicate what he or she feels most familiar with. The Bible is therefore not only the "source" for the gospel message, it is also the means by which we are able to imagine this message expressed differently.

An intimate knowledge of culture is also required to share the Christian faith with young people. This sensitivity only comes from time spent with groups and individuals. Translation happens when the youthworker begins to look through the glasses of young people's culture at the Bible. This again is largely a matter of imagination and trial and error. Looking through the glasses means that we bring the life experiences, questions, and values of the group to the biblical material. Translation also means looking from the Bible to the young people's lives and from young people's lives to the Bible. The question which the youthworker has to keep in the forefront of his or her mind will be, "What is the good news for this group?"

What is good news depends upon what aspect of the gospel story brings God's life to young people. It is this good news which must be proclaimed. The youthworker is the means by which young people initially hear the translated message. The translation of the message is not an academic exercise—it is essentially practical. In the first instance it affects the way youthwork is carried out in practice (for more on this see Chapter 6). How we do youthwork should be shaped by what we think is good news for the young people we are working with. Christian youthwork can be very diverse: for instance, it can focus around the offer of support or it can primarily concern itself with challenge; it can be mainly spiritual or it can have an emphasis upon social concern; it can be based in a locality or it can bring young people together from around the world. Each of these possibilities (and of course there are a good many more than these), might be good news to different groups of young people. It is the job of translation to make the right choice of style of youthwork practice. A major criticism of Christian youthwork is that it very rarely shapes its practice around a concern to be good news among a particular group of young people. More often than not the style of a youthwork project arises because it is perceived to be successful elsewhere. Youthwork in this way spreads by one group copying another. An incarnational approach to youthwork will put a high priority on shaping the work around a faithfulness to the Bible and a sensitivity to the subculture of a particular group of young people. Ideas gleaned elsewhere should be judged in light of this.

Christian youthworkers are called to proclaim the gospel in both word and deed. Telling the gospel message to a group of unchurched young people can be very challenging. Most youthworkers feel a certain anxiety when they come to talk about the Christian faith for the first time. Some of this anxiety comes because in past experience most of us have seen young people respond negatively to an overt preaching of the gospel. These kinds of negative experiences, however, generally come about where Christians have tried to preach the gospel to young people they don't know or in situations in which the young people feel that the message is inappropriate. The challenge for the incarnational worker is to use a close knowledge of the culture of the young people to overcome these problems.

In the first instance the successful translator of the gospel will be the person who finds a situation where the young people themselves are open to hearing the message. This means that the group will need to feel that they are consulted about the introduction of stories about Jesus. It could be that the best approach to this is for the youthworker to make storytelling a normal part of the contact work with the group. Telling the gospel story then becomes a steady and natural part of the life of the group. The key in doing this, however, lies in finding a way of telling the story that does not seem forced or out of order to the group.

Having found the right situation, the youthworker decides what is best to be said. In many situations the young people will have no knowledge of the Bible or of the Christian faith. The youthworker thus has the responsibility to choose the kind of Bible-based message that will make sense in the young people's lives. Inspiration for this process can be drawn from published interpretations of the Bible such as Eugene Petersen's *The Message* and Walter Wangerin's *The Book of*

God.[4] In most cases it is inappropriate to simply lift passages from these kinds of books. Both Wangerin and Petersen, although very talented, are conditioned by their own cultural setting. What works for white middle-aged men may not be the best translation for groups of young people. The best approach is for the youthworker to use these versions of the Bible as a guide and an inspiration. Reading a passage in *The Message* or *The Book of God* can give the youthworker a new angle on a biblical passage and begin to spark new thoughts for a dynamic translation which is rooted in the experience and lives of particular groups of young people.

♦*Incarnation of the Word in the Lives of Young People*

The eventual aim of youth ministry should be that young people begin to develop the faith within their own cultural world. When young people hear and respond to the message translated into their world through the words and the actions of youthworkers and other members of the church, a new situation arises. The young people who have newly come to faith are able to access the Bible for themselves. The hope is that they do this while remaining within their own subculture. For some young people reading the Bible will be a distinct possibility, especially if they are introduced to one of the more readable modern translations. My own current favorite is the Contemporary English Version, which is produced in England by the Bible Society. The advantage of this text, which was first designed to be read out loud, is that it follows the rhythms of modern speech. This means that it tends to make sense to the everyday reader on first sight. It also has the advantage of keeping to a relatively simple vocabulary. For a good many other young people, reading may not be the best way of accessing the biblical material. The youthworker in this situation will need to continue as storyteller. This can be substituted by using videos which portray the gospel in drama. The *Jesus of Nazareth* series is a good resource in this respect.

However the biblical material is put into the hands of the young people, the role of the youthworker is to act as guide to the group. Space for discussion and for prayer means that young people can begin to process the stories from the Bible into practical Christian discipleship within their own context. The hope is that they develop an approach to being Christian and to believing that is indigenous to their youth subculture. As more young people begin to join in with this process, a new Christian community starts to emerge (how this community begins to find a worshiping life of its own is explored in more depth in Chapter 7).

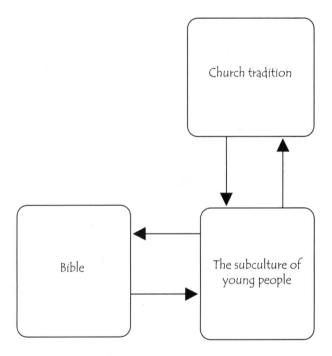

The Limitations of Contextualization ◆◆◆◆◆◆◆◆

There are dangers in any contextualization of the gospel. The desire is that the Christian faith is incarnated within the subculture of a group of young people. Unfortunately, it is possible for this process to go astray. It is a major temptation to so accommodate the gospel to the culture of the group that essential aspects of the Christian message can become blunted. For instance, the desire to make the gospel attractive may play down the demand for personal or for social morality. Dietrich Bonhoeffer warned the church of the dangers of cheap grace, that is, the offer of God's blessing and acceptance without the demands of following Christ. Bonhoeffer's message in *The Cost of Discipleship* sounds a note of warning to youthworkers today, just as it did to the German church in the 1930s.[5] The story of the cooperation of the church with a pagan and even occult Nazi state in Germany is a salutary warning for any contextualization today.

Young people seeking a path of Christian discipleship need to hear the voices of others within the Christian tradition to keep them on the track. It is the task of the youthworker and other mature Christians involved with the group to bring into the creative contextualizing process the wisdom that is in the history and tradition of the church. The road to working out the faith in a new cultural setting is lined with blind alleys. The history of the church gives evidence of the temptation to accommodate the gospel to one's own culture or to make of the God of the Bible a tame replica who affirms everything one thinks or does. This kind of comfortable accommodation has been a feature of church history and indeed of present-day church culture, and there is no reason to believe that young people are immune to this temptation. Young people need the insights that come from the history of the wider church to bring a sense of balance and maturity to their pilgrimage. True contextualization requires a rootedness in culture, a faithfulness to the Bible, and an openness to the tradition of the church.

Questions to Ponder and Discuss

1. How central is the incarnation to the whole argument of this book? How is the idea used in the first four chapters? What is being added here? How does the cultural world of the Bible relate to our cultural world? How do the cultural worlds of young people relate to your cultural world? What does this chapter provide as the key to resolving these tensions?

2. In order to translate the Bible properly, missionaries have been forced to consider (a) the culture of the people, (b) their own culture, and (c) the culture of the Bible. Using this model, what must we take seriously in communicating the Bible to young people in a today's world?

3. What new thoughts has this chapter stimulated in you? What impresses and helps you most? Are there any with which you disagree?

4. What might be some dangers or limitations of contextualization and cultural sensitivity? What would you add to or emphasize from this chapter?

Getting Started:
Two Case Studies

Evangelicals have tended to think of the gospel as a series of propositions. Each proposition leads logically on to the next. Thus an evangelistic presentation will consist of a series of statements. To lead someone to Christ involves a process of moving the person through this sequence. A simple summary of the gospel might read like this.

a) We are fallen and sinful and therefore separated from God.

b) Jesus died for our sins on the cross to bring us back to God.

c) To be reunited with God we must ask for forgiveness of our sins, accept that Jesus died for us, and receive his forgiveness.

It is possible to critique this kind of presentation. One way would be to indicate that the presentation of the gospel in these statements is incomplete in some way. Some would, for instance, want to start the explanation of the gospel with a statement that gives prominence to God's love for humanity as part of creation. This would be expressed as a theological argument that the gospel story places a prior emphasis upon creation rather than upon the fall. This may or may not be the case, but what we should also bear in mind is that the first proposition in a linear understanding of the gospel will tend to determine how we relate to people whom we are seeking to introduce to the faith. Our starting point of a linear understanding of the gospel is therefore the kind of doorway through which we hope people will pass as they become Christians. If we see the entry point to the linear sequence as human sinfulness, then we will be wanting to "convict" people of sin. If, however, we see the starting point as the love of God, then we will tend to find ways to express this insight by being warm and accepting. For the youthworker seeking to contextualize the gospel in the lives of young people, the linear model of presenting the message has significant problems.

Linear summaries of the gospel tend to simplify biblical narrative. In the three-point outline, for instance, the meaning of Christ's death on the cross has been expressed solely in terms of a sacrifice for sin. In contrast it is possible to see in the biblical material and in the tradition of the church a number of different understandings of the death of Christ.[1] Christians have at different times responded to Christ's death as a victory over death or evil; others have been moved by the self-giving of Christ to follow a new way of life; and more recently the suffering of Christ has been expounded as an identification with the suffering of humanity. The gospel is a complex story that carries within it a number of different and complementary meanings. The summary I have presented above is not necessarily wrong, but it is just *one* possible route of interpretation through the gospel narrative. For those involved in communicating the faith to young people, a simple presentation of the gospel has always been attractive. The problem is that reliance upon one expression of the message reduces the number of available interpretations.

Sharing the faith across cultures and subcultures requires us to keep an open mind regarding two characteristics of the gospel. First we need to see that there are many possible doorways into the faith. Second, we must acknowledge that there are a number of legitimate interpretations of key moments in the gospel narrative, such as the cross of Christ or the nature and effect of human sinfulness. These two considerations mean that a reductive linear construction of theological propositions is severely limited for Christian youthwork. A more helpful understanding of the gospel might be to see theological truth as a three-dimensional honeycomb or cluster of ideas. Any one of the key ideas within the honeycomb can act as an entry point or doorway. Instead of a linear progression of the gospel narrative with a prescribed order for understanding of the message, a honeycomb approach would see understanding as developing in a more organic way, from one cell of the honeycomb to another. Full Christian discipleship comes only when all of the key cells in the honeycomb are understood and incorporated into the lives and culture of the young people who are coming to faith. This conception of the gospel affirms that youthworkers will want to live out the gospel among young people in a variety of different ways, depending upon the subculture they are working within. This understanding of the faith also means that in speaking about the gospel the youthworker can start with the part of the honeycomb that is most appropriate to the context of the group. At the same time the honeycomb concept will act as a reminder that the Christian faith must be encountered as a network of truths and interpretations of the gospel.

Andrew Walker's description of the gospel as "Grand Narrative of the Christian people" complements the honeycomb idea. For Walker, evangelism is the process by which the gospel comes alive for us, the process of seeing our own lives as part of the grand story of God.[2] Stories engage different people in different ways. We are caught up in the narrative when we begin to identify with particular moments within the story. In other words, there are different parts of the story that ring true for different groups of people, different cultures and subcultures. The narrative pattern of the gospel, however, demands that for a complete understanding of the story of God—and indeed of ourselves—we need to ultimately engage with the full flow of the story. We can get in touch with the story by starting at a number of different points, but to be part of God's story we need the whole plot. Eventually the entire honeycomb needs to be explored; the whole of the narrative needs to become a place of identity and meaning for those coming to faith. The key factor in how this comes about will be what is chosen as the starting point in the honeycomb or in the story. It is the starting point that locates the practice of youthwork within the gospel story (or places it within the honeycomb). Christian youthwork that is committed to the gospel must be shaped by an appreciation of the importance of this starting point.

This chapter presents two case studies. The case studies describe the social situation of two different groups of young people who live in the same town. First the social world of the group is described. The gospel is then looked at to see what a possible starting point for a contextual mission might be with this group. Finally in the light of the social context of the group and the chosen starting point within the gospel story, an approach to youth ministry among the group is set out. These case studies are fictional constructions; however, they are based upon the work of successive groups of students at Oxford Youth Works who each year study real groups of young people and follow a similar pattern of contextual theologizing.

Case Study One ◆◆◆◆◆◆◆◆◆◆◆◆◆◆◆◆◆◆◆◆◆◆◆◆◆

This group of fourteen-year-olds have all grown up in a predominately blue-collar neighborhood. Their parents are in and out of work, mostly in low-paying, entry-level jobs. A number of the youth come from fairly dysfunctional families and some come from single-parent homes. The group all attend school, but they are not among the most academically successful. They expect to leave high school with very few qualifications, and they know that means career-oriented jobs will be hard to come by.

Everyone in this group dresses similarly. They wear what are considered mainstream clothes at their school: baggy jeans, baggy cotton shirts, basketball shoes or workboots with loose laces. Particular attention is paid to the make of their shoes, and at this moment in time they favor Fila and Timberlane. The boys wear baseball caps high on their head, backward. The logo on the caps in most cases reads "Chicago Bulls." The girls have elaborate hairstyles, make-up, and jewelry. Their clothes closely resemble those of the boys, although sometimes their shirts are more form-fitting. Boys and girls both have tattoos and body piercings. The individuals in the group are not particularly communicative, however, they will talk at some length about their latest sexual exploits or of the latest gang-related happenings. Some of the group have been involved in illegal activities, a few have been arrested for alcohol and drug related offenses, and one has been arrested for car theft.

Trouble seems a feature of the lives of many of those in the group. One reason for this is their attitude. They all share an anti-authoritarian stance when it comes to the police, school, and even some of their parents. They get into trouble fairly regularly, but confrontation with authority is not seen as an end in itself by the group. They regard trouble with the police or with the school as a natural (most have a friend or relative in prison), and possibly unfortunate, consequence of the activities they choose to indulge in. The group shares a tight friendship with each other based on shared activities and possibly arising from the reaction they inspire in others. They have an acute sense of group loyalty. The unforgivable sin is to squeal on someone. Nonetheless, each of the individuals shows signs of a lack of self-esteem. The friendship of the group helps to compensate for this.

♦ The Good News for the Group

The gospels show Jesus taking particular notice of those who were on the underside of his society. The good news is to be proclaimed to the "poor."[3] Jesus seems to have made a particular point of eating with and socializing with those groups who were disadvantaged or who lacked choices. At one point Jesus is questioned about the company he keeps.

> And the Pharisees and their scribes murmured against his disciples, saying, "Why do you eat and drink with tax collectors and sinners?" And Jesus answered them, "Those who are well have no need of a physician, but those who are sick; I have not come to call the righteous, but sinners to repentance."[4]

Those regarded as sinners were the people who, for one reason or another, were unable to keep the complex web of purity laws followed by the Pharisees. Joachim Jeremias calls these the "people of the land,"[5] the ones who worked for a living but whose work kept them out of synagogue life. For instance, those working with animals would of necessity come into contact on a daily basis with animal dung, or other material. Under Jewish purity laws this would make them ritually unclean and exclude them from worship. The people of the land therefore were those who were outside the acceptable world of Jewish religious life, and yet Jesus built relationships with them. Edward Schillebeeckx sees the "table fellowship" of Christ as a portent of God's coming kingdom. By eating and drinking with sinners Jesus brings the possibility of new life and signals a freedom.[6] The kingdom of God is a great feast where in the absence of the invited guests the roads are searched for those who are hanging around. In this sweep both the good and the bad enter in.[7]

In the gospels we see Jesus developing a particular relationship with the people of the land. Like the young people in the case study, they lived on the margins of acceptable behavior, sometimes inside the law and sometimes outside it. Jesus is clear that they are sinners and that they need the healing work of the doctor, but he appears to be willing to compromise his religious identity and respectability in order to bring the kingdom to them. Moreover, while repentance and new life are seen to come from these encounters, what evidence we have of this seems to confound the expectations of the religious community.

It is the presence of Christ among the people of the land which brings about change and renewal. Tax collectors, prostitutes, and political rebels are all turned around by relationship with Jesus. These people were seen as lacking in social worth by the religious people of the day. In contrast Jesus offers the high honor of sharing meals, and he invites them to join his fellowship of followers. These people may well have been outsiders to the synagogue, but they had a place in the kingdom which Jesus came to proclaim. There are moments when the warmth of relationship and of encounter between Jesus and the people of the land is a disturbing sign of the coming kingdom. An example of this is the time Jesus is dining with a Pharisee and a prostitute gate-crashes the evening and starts to weep at Jesus' feet, wetting his feet and wiping the tears away with her hair.[8] The intimacy of this encounter is a powerful sign of the coming kingdom and a rebuke to the Pharisee, as Jesus points out.

. . . Do you see this woman? I entered your house, you gave me no water for my feet, but she has wet my feet with her tears and wiped them with her hair. You gave me no kiss, but from the time I came in she has not ceased to kiss my feet. You did not anoint my head with oil, but she has anointed my feet with ointment.[9]

The behavior of the woman in the society of the day was outrageous. Any respectable religious person would have been offended. It is possible that despite this the Pharisee in the story is embarrassed into inaction by the affrontery of the woman. She is a righteous rebel in that her faithfulness calls the Pharisee's religious commitment into question.

◆The Way In for Youthwork

In the gospels we see Jesus making a point of spending time with the people of the land. Incarnational youthwork would see the importance of this kind of contact ministry, but not simply as a technique of reaching out to young people. Contact work for this group is the key method of sharing the good news. The lack of self-worth and the compensatory behavior and identity of the group mean that the youthworker must also identify strongly with the young people. The example of sharing meals seen in the gospel record of the life of Jesus can be paralleled by the many occasions where the group "hangs out" on the street corner. Identification will not involve approval of car theft or any other illegal activity, but it might leave some room for acknowledgement of the skill, energy, and organization involved in stealing a car, however misdirected those efforts have been. Enthusiasm for cars might be a starting point for extended contact with the group. The priority, however, will be to make sure that these young people experience the "love" of God through the ongoing presence of the youthworker in the life of the group.

When it comes to sharing the gospel story, a major priority should be placed on presenting Jesus as a working man who identified with those who were similar in class and background to himself. This Jesus is one who spoke with the slang of his region, who had time for the outsider, who was not soft on wrongdoing, but who always made space to spend time with his friends. The distant church that speaks in four-syllable words needs to be corrected by a vision of a Jesus who himself spoke and behaved in a normal everyday way. The love of God seen in the caring work of the youthworker and in the story of the gospel needs to be the recurring theme of the proclamation. The youth need to feel that God values them and that he is very much concerned with what they want to do with their lives. God is on their side.

The loyalty of the group offers a sign of the kingdom of God. Jesus also had a group of close friends. They went off on trips together, just like the group does. The disciples were Jesus' special friends who shared his mission and his lifestyle. Jesus was the kind of person who was there for his friends when times were tough. But he was the kind of friend who let you know what the score was. Jesus was straightforward and honest, and if the disciples were out of line, then he let them know it. The difference for Jesus and the disciples is that they were involved in living for God's kingdom. This is quite different from stealing cars. The disciples' identity was linked to their relationship to Jesus, not to their feelings at that time. This kind of connection needs to be made for the young people to respond to the love of God.

Following Christ should also be linked to the clear need for these young people to find jobs. Jobs give not only money, but they often give identity and self-worth. To be earning good money is to have made it. Youthwork must not be a distraction from this process. Discipleship must be linked to helping young people move into adulthood, which means moving into work or training for work. This might mean supporting members of the group as they begin studies at the community college; it might mean that every week the group prays for aspects of training and applying for work. The youth minister may go further and become personally involved in finding or creating jobs. In all of this, faith in Christ and moving on in life need to be explicitly linked.

Faith in Christ does not mean fitting into a Christian middle-class stereotype. It is possible to be outrageous to religious people in the way we worship God and express our relationship with him. The group need to see that Jesus wants them to be natural in their fellowship and in their church life.

This might, for instance, mean that when they pray they occasionally use swear words, or at the worship time they allow smoking, or they invite only working-class people to speak at the worship. All of these would be fairly shocking within a church setting, but for this group they may be an aspect of contextualization within culture which is simply natural as well as being outrageous. Like the woman who washed Jesus' feet with her tears, these young people will be trying to be Christians the best way that they can. Their actions may cause offense, but that is just part of faithfulness to Christ.

Case Study Two ◆◆◆◆◆◆◆◆◆◆◆◆◆◆◆◆◆◆◆◆◆◆◆◆◆◆

This group of ten young people come from a well-to-do part of town. The young people in the group all live in large, nicely landscaped houses. In all but one case the young people live with both of their natural parents. The parents of the group all work in middle-class or professional occupations, e.g., professors, lawyers, doctors, or middle managers.

The group are seen by themselves and by the other staff and pupils in the school as the successful "in crowd." They occupy the central table in the school cafeteria most lunch times. They are noisy and full of jokes. Being around them is fun. They are attractive, open, and welcoming, but also a little intimidating for the outsider to join. They all expect to do well at school and to go on to a good college. In general the ambitions of the group are toward high-profile, well-paid jobs that offer a challenge and interesting life: working in the media, running their own business, and being a sports physiotherapist, for example. They are aiming for success and they are expected to achieve it. Pressure to succeed comes not only from their homes but also from the school, whose prestige is partly dependent upon these students doing well on standardized tests and getting into well-known colleges.

All of the group work on Saturdays and on occasional evenings. They are therefore extremely busy, but on Saturday night they party. All of the group have false IDs, which they use to buy alcohol. They get together at hangout spots in the woods or at someone's house, where they drink a lot and "get trashed." This is their way of letting off steam. They are also fairly regular drug users, smoking marijuana on the weekends. Their parents and the school are basically aware of what the group does. The agreement seems to be that if they get their school work done and continue to do well, then what they do on weekends is their own business.

The conversation within the group is extremely superficial, rarely moving out of joking and goofing around. The group has no sense of any real problems in life. If they have problems they all feel able to talk with their parents or with the staff at school, whom they find to be approachable and helpful.

◆The **G**oo*d* *New*s for the **G**r**o**up

The doorway to the gospel for this group cannot be based upon any sense of need, or indeed sinfulness. The loving caring presence of a youthworker may well be welcomed, but any depth of relationship might prove very difficult. The members of the group are so secure in their successful path through school and on into adult life that they have little need of another adult person with whom to share their troubles. Contact work alone, therefore, will leave the youthworker with a good deal of fun interaction with the group, but very little progress. The youthworker who sees himself or herself as someone offering care in answer to need will find that there is no way into the gospel honeycomb for this group. A more appropriate expression of the gospel might start with a commitment to challenge the priorities of the group.

The parable of the talents represents the kingdom of God as being related to the responsible and entrepreneurial use of gifts and abilities to bring about economic success.[10] The servants in the story are given differing amounts of money according to their abilities. When the master returns they are called to account for what they have done with this money, and they are rewarded for making a hefty profit. The message is that the kingdom of God is related to the responsible use of God-given prosperity and opportunity. Those who are given a great deal are expected to produce a great deal. Prosperity in itself, however, is not really the goal. The story of the rich man who tore down his barns to build bigger ones strikes a warning note.

> And he said, "I will do this: I will pull down my barns, and build larger ones; and there I will store all my grain and my goods. And I will say to my soul, Soul, you have ample goods laid up for many years; take your ease, eat, drink, be merry." But God said to him, "Fool! This night your soul is required of you; and the things you have prepared, whose will they be?" So is he who lays up treasure for himself, and is not rich toward God.[11]

Making it in the kingdom involves working for God. This means using the gifts and abilities that God has given us to achieve great things for God, not necessarily for our own pleasure or enjoyment. The call of the disciples gives another clue to this.[12] The disciples were asked by Jesus, "Follow me." This meant a costly turning away from their previous life and entering another much more challenging one. Jesus asks every Christian to make a difference in the world, but those who have much are expected to give the most. Tony Campolo has developed an approach to youthwork in a US context where many Christian young people are privileged and wealthy. He points out that young people are turned on by challenge. It is in this way, he says, that evangelistic organizations have inspired thousands of young people to set out to try to "convert the world for Christ." A seemingly otherworldly invitation to reach beyond ourselves is very attractive. To be an entrepreneur for the kingdom of God brings out heroism among young people. Campolo sees that there is much to be learned from the idea of a holy crusade, and many young people are yearning for a way to make a mark in the world. To do this at the invitation of God and in God's name is a radical and dynamic lifestyle choice for young people and one that is very attractive.[13]

♦The Way In for Youthwork

The call to follow Christ, therefore, should start with the challenge to live a different life. The focus for this group should not be on the needs of the young people, whether these be seen as social or spiritual. These young people are winners wanting to make their mark in life. They want to be creative and businesslike. The key message is that these things of themselves are God-given desires and talents. The question is, to what ends are they going to give their lives? The youthworker needs to devise a strategy to offer radical new options to the group for heroic service in the cause of the kingdom of God. These young people are ambitious; the task of the youthworker is to show how God wants them to use their talents positively for him.

Repentance therefore takes the form of challenging the group to choose a new kind of lifestyle. This does not mean an undue attention on the recreational use of alcohol or drugs, however wrong this might be. The starting point must be the presentation of other attractive options for giving their lives in the service of God and other people. One option could be to introduce the group to Christians who are running their own businesses. Work experience schemes give the chance for young people in their later years at school to spend time with companies and businesses. A placement with Christians running or working in a media or publicity company might offer an insight into a creative use of energy which operates within a Christian framework. The role of the youthworker is not just to set up this kind of opportunity but also to spend time with individuals talking through what they have experienced. The gospel implications of what the young people are experiencing can then be unpacked and worked through. How Christ fits the challenge to achieve something in life can become an overt part of the discussion.

Another approach might be to take the group on a trip abroad to see how Christian charities are working with people in the two-thirds world through projects such as an income generation scheme. This kind of small investment use of capital to stimulate business among groups of poor people to whom the banks have been reluctant to lend can offer an inspiring example of how the young people themselves can make a difference by using their own gifts and skills. The Christian context of these kinds of charitable initiatives offer the occasion for the youthworker to speak of Jesus as someone who calls us to follow him by giving our lives in similar efforts to make the world a better place. Campolo has devised schemes whereby relatively wealthy young people spend time working alongside Christians who are caring for the poor.

The example of self-giving lives that are filled with prayer and spiritual energy in the face of awful suffering raises questions in the minds of these young people. According to Campolo, this kind of challenge to service in the kingdom evangelizes young people in ways that the need approach to the gospel rarely touches.[14]

These case studies offer an insight into the way that specific youthwork projects can be fundamentally shaped by both the call of the gospel and the social context of young people.[15] The process of getting close to a group and reading the gospel through their eyes allows us to see the way that missiological insights into translating the gospel can reshape the way youthwork is done. This approach can be adopted both for work Outside-In and for work that is Inside-Out. The second case study has particular relevance for more privileged church young people who may have grown somewhat complacent about the faith.

Questions to Ponder and Discuss

1. What do you think about the following statements?

   Youth ministry in America has been tilted toward the middle class. You can tell this by looking at the youth magazines and curriculum, training materials, and camps. A second priority, far down the line, has been urban, particularly African-American young people. Other ethnicities, rural youth, and blue-collar young people have largely been ignored.

2. This chapter presents an opportunity to consider how ministries with blue-collar and middle-class suburban kids must differ. In what way are all young people and ministry with them the same? In what ways do kids differ, and how must our ministry adapt to various subcultures and lifestyles?

3. What challenges you most from this chapter? How is your experience similar to or different from the author's?

Chapter 7

Youth Ministry and the Church

Youth ministry starts and ends with the church. At first this may not appear entirely obvious. If we are honest we will recognize that youth activities have often been an escape, for leaders and for young people, from regular Sunday worship or Sunday school. To compensate for a lack of enthusiasm about church services, youth ministers plan activities that are more in touch with the culture of young people, activities that cater to their musical tastes and desire for informality. To youth ministers this youth-oriented world that we create often seems more relevant and certainly more alive than the worship service held every Sunday morning. In fact, for many young people and youth leaders "church" is something that is endured rather than enjoyed. And youth ministers often tend to be critical or uncomfortable with traditional Sunday worship. "It's not really for us—it's for the older folk. Given the choice we would do something very different!" This same response to many aspects of congregational life has fostered a "culture of escape" among youth ministers.

One way that youth ministry has escaped from "church" is through separate parachurch organizations. For those involved in these organizations their relationship with church may seem much simpler. There are no clear organizational links between youth organizations such as Young Life or Youth For Christ and denominational groups. Youth ministers work for the organization rather than any individual church. This type of arrangement offers a good deal of freedom, since parachurch agencies are not obliged to connect young people with a particular congregation. For them the numbers of young people in Sunday School or at worship on a Sunday morning is not the measure of success—as it would definitely be for the youth minister employed by the local congregation. Parachurch youth agencies tend to make the church attractive to young people by concentrating solely on their needs. How young people actually connect with church congregational life lies outside the scope of parachurch activity—and perhaps interest.

Escape Is Futile ◆◆◆◆◆◆◆◆◆◆◆◆◆◆◆◆◆◆◆◆◆◆◆◆◆◆◆

However much we try to escape, youth ministry remains irrevocably connected to the church universal. The youth minister may not actually work for a particular congregation or denominational organization but the running costs of the ministry, and possibly the salary, are met by the faithful giving of Christian people. At a very basic level the Christian community pays the bills. It is my view that this financial connection between the ministry and Christian people is a spiritual one. The ties that develop between ministry and supporters are a witness to the deeper spiritual connection we have in Christ.

As youth ministers we are well aware that our work is done in the name of Jesus. We know that it is the power of the Holy Spirit that enables us to care for young people. Our self-understanding is often linked to our sense of a "call." We may well say to ourselves when things get tough, "Jesus has challenged me to work among young people in this town and so that's what I must do." One of the problems with this is that we easily fall into the mistake of seeing our vocation in purely individual terms. We fail to see how our sense of calling relates to the wider Christian community.

Youth ministry grows from a partnership in the gospel. Those working with young people and those who support that work (if they are believers) are participating in the activity of the body of Christ. This is a spiritual thing—it's about the way that Jesus works through his community in a particular place to bring about the kingdom. We need to remind ourselves on a regular basis of this gospel truth—we are part of the body of Christ. The body of Christ is, of course, the Christian church past present and future. This again is a spiritual reality but it is played out in the various denominations, congregations, and fellowships that form part of the religious pattern of the contemporary church. I am not arguing for any particular church organization or denomination, rather, my point is that we are connected, because we are united in Jesus Christ. The specifics of how this works out will be different in every country, city, and neighborhood, but the gospel dynamic is essentially the same. If we are faithful to Jesus we cannot regard ourselves as disconnected from his body. As Paul says:

> A body isn't really a body, unless there is more than one part. It takes many parts to make a single body. That's why the eyes cannot say they don't need the hands. That's also why the head cannot say it doesn't need the feet. (1 Cor 12:19–20 Contemporary English Version)

Another way to look at the body of Christ is through our own personal histories. If we are involved in all kinds of innovative youth programs at this present time, we have become so almost certainly through the Christian church. The gospel is communicated through the witness of Christians who have gone before us. For most of us this connection will have been played out through some connection with a congregation in our home town or through a Christian group in our school or at college. In these instances the body of Christ is very visible and we are well aware that we owe our faith to others and this gives us a sense of identity and belonging. Even for those of us whose faith has come through a more individualistic experience—reading the Bible, or praying—we are still affected somewhere along the line by the presence, words, or writings of the Christian community.

It is a profound and at times uncomfortable truth that our Christian faith does not rest totally in a personal relationship with Jesus. For to know Jesus is to be connected through him to his body—the church. For those of us engaged in reaching out to young people this connectedness is hard to shake off.

However much we feel marginalized or organizationally disconnected from denominational structures or particular communities we are drawn back into relationship with them because our mission among young people is not our own: it is God's. Our call to care for young people is located in the wider purposes of God and so however much we may try to escape the gospel draws us into relationship with the body of Christ—the church. If we try to escape this fact then we separate ourselves from the purposes of God and deny something of who we are. Escape is futile.

Young People Need the Church ♦♦♦♦♦♦♦♦♦♦♦♦♦

Youth ministry starts with the church because a youth minister's self-understanding originates in the body of Christ and the mission of God. Youth ministry, however, also should find its end in the church. In reaching out to young people our desire is to see them begin to develop a relationship with Jesus Christ. The logic of this is that through their encounter with Jesus young Christian people are part of the body of Christ.

The problem youth ministry faces is how to enable young people to develop a connection between their experience of Jesus and the concrete expression of his body in our local neighborhood. A youth ministry that does not take seriously this aspect of the work is severely flawed, both theologically and practically. It propagates an incomplete gospel and, it does not provide for young people who are growing in their faith a place of ongoing mature community. The bottom line is that youth ministry cannot escape the church because young people need the church to become faithful disciples.

It is my belief that distinguishing between the two different types of youth ministry—Inside-Out and Outside-In—is necessary for helping young people form healthy, long-term relationships with local Christian communities. The kind of model which we are operating needs to be understood by the congregation, its leaders, and the youth minister involved. This is the first key stage in developing an effective and long-term relationship between the ministry and the local congregation.

Relating to Church—Inside-Out ◆◆◆◆◆◆◆◆◆◆◆◆◆◆

The nucleus-fringe, or Inside-Out, model of youth ministry is built around a group of young people who themselves are already Christian. These young people generally come from Christian families. And even if they do not attend church, they are connected to Christian communities. The nucleus approach builds on this group's Christian commitment and understanding, which they inherently gain from their families and from the wider Christian community. The social dynamic of relationship between a nucleus group and the Christian church is inherent to the model. It is built in.

The nucleus group may appear to be very different from the rest of the church in the way it organizes its activities. Its style of worship, Bible study, and Christian service may seem radical and out of step with regular church life. Indeed, youth ministry has often set itself the task of generating an innovative culture. But however new and exciting the program may be, it is still undeniably built upon the beliefs, traditions, and ministries of parent congregations. The youth ministry may share with the parent church a commitment to a common core of Christian truth understood in a particular way. In addition to this the youth ministry may be innovative but it does this in relation to the parent congregation. By its reaction to the adult congregation, a youth ministry expresses difference while at the same time confirming continuity.

Working Inside-Out means that we should never underestimate the commonalities that exist between our activities and the local church. For while we may feel that we are doing something new and different, we are always operating in relation to the established Christian community. My own view is that the function of the nucleus group is to develop the future culture of the church. What happens in the youth group today will be happening in the rest of the church in ten or so years. "Radical" styles of worship very soon become the dominant culture in the church. Today's young people become the church leaders and congregational members of tomorrow, and as they grow up they take their culture—albeit mellowed and adapted—with them. The songs we sing in church today have come out of the Jesus movement of the late 1960s and early

1970s. Church culture is far from static; indeed, contemporary media has quickened the pace at which the church continually adapts innovations originating in youth ministry.

The Inside-Out approach is built upon the assumption that a church's young people will remain connected to their parent congregation. The health of the church and the stability of its youth ministry require a relationship and flow of ideas between these two groups. However uncomfortable the older members of the congregation may be with the young people and however impatient young people may be with the rest of the church, they still need each other. They are all part of the body of Christ and therefore interdependent.

While this interdependence must be acknowledged and fostered, young people must be allowed to develop a separate identity and cultural distance from the rest of the church. A distinct Sunday school class or youth worship service or congregation allows young people to begin to experiment with expressions of the faith that connect with their own cultural setting. In the United Kingdom over the last five years we have seen an incredible move of God among Christian young people that has been characterized by new forms of worship. In many towns and cities its is now common to find youth services run entirely by young people. Some of these gatherings of young Christians would call themselves youth congregations or even youth churches. In most cases they have come into existence with the blessing and support of local congregations and they maintain a link with older congregations in a variety of ways. Many come under the eldership of the minister, but they meet separately. Some have attracted a mixed age range, but leadership is in the hands of young people or young adults. In some cases joint services are run with the young people and older congregations sharing their styles of worship with each other.

These developments are very much at an experimental stage. No two youth congregations are alike. How they relate to the local congregations and the wider church appears to be slightly different with each group. At the one end of the spectrum there are groups which are essentially church youth fellowships which worship in their own meetings. They see Sunday worship as valuable but perhaps not essential on a weekly basis. At the other end of the spectrum there are youth churches: free standing new congregations who control their own finances and appoint their own ministers. Between these extremes there are any number of different arrangements.

What is exciting about these developments is that young people are being allowed to find space to express the faith in their own cultural ways. They have not done this by separating entirely from the older congregation. They have instead sought to find ways to negotiate a place alongside the local church. It is this mix of independence and interdependence that must continue to characterize the youth ministry of the future.

Relating to Church—Outside-In ♦♦♦♦♦♦♦♦♦♦♦♦♦♦

Church is also of the utmost importance for the Outside-In model of youth ministry. The model starts with incarnational relationships that are developed within the cultural world of a group of young people. Their aim is to see this group begin to experience the love of Christ and then come to faith. A weakness of this method is that a relationship with a church is not part of the natural social dynamic of the group. Much of the group may not have family connections with local churches. This means that such a relationship has to be set up—this is far from easy.

Many churches are willing to be welcoming to their own young people, however strange they may appear to be. With those young people with whom they have little or no social connection, however, there is an unfortunate tendency to be less sympathetic. I have had many disappointing experiences along these lines. Just about every month I get a call from a youthworker who cannot find a congregation that will accept a group of young people. Many churches want to protect their own young people and keep the church as a safe space. Sadly, they try to do this by pushing away "outsider" young people who are seen a problem or a threat by parents and the wider congregation.

It is part of the task of youth ministry to act as advocate of these young people. We need to work with church leaders, elders, and members of the congregation to find ways in which young people, however undisciplined and unchurched they

may be, will be accepted. Young people who are in a relationship with Jesus Christ are part of the body of Christ. It is a
gospel imperative that the church welcome them, even if it requires some bending. The youth too, must be willing to be re-
spectful of the values and traditions of the church. Thus both
the church and the youth must work towards a balanced,
healthy interdependence.

At the same time the youth minister must realize that
these young people need a degree of independence; they need
the space to develop their own styles of worship and Christian
expression. Cultural space is as important for young people
who are coming through the Outside-In model as it is for those
who are part of an Inside-Out nucleus group. In this respect
these "outsider" groups are much more needy, because of their
distinctive culture. The aim should be for the group to develop
an expression of the faith that will in time grow into a coherent
church life. The young people will eventually grow up and
probably have kids of their own. In England there are a number of youth congregations that are slowly turning into fully-
fledged intergenerational churches. As the young Christians
that belong to these youth congregations get married and
have children, these churches grow. The church continues to
grow as they witness to their families and members of their
community.

The Bottom Line for Youth Ministry and the Church ◆◆◆◆◆◆◆◆◆◆◆◆◆◆◆◆◆◆◆◆◆◆◆◆◆

The bottom line for youth ministry is that it really must
start to take the whole idea of church much more seriously.
How this plays out in each setting will be very different, but my
sense is that we need to work at the relationship. That said it is
also true that leaders, congregations, denominations—in fact
any level of church—has a similar task on its hands. If the
young people and youth ministry in general need to foster positive connections with the various aspects of congregational/
church life the same is true on the other side of the fence.

It is my view that these discussions could be helped considerably if they are based on common expectations and theoretical frameworks. Part of the problem, in my experience, in negotiations between youth ministry and churches is simple misunderstanding. We don't really share a common language about the work which we are trying to do. Partly this is because youth ministers are more inclined to be activists than theorists, but my sense is that very often youth ministry is innovative, on the cutting edge, and so it is sometimes hard to express exactly what is going on and how it relates to the existing life of the church.

One of the chief reasons for writing this book has been to try to put into words a basic theory for understanding youth ministry. My aim has been to express what I see as the strategic and theoretical fault line which divides the different traditions of working with young people. While I realize that every situation is different and has its own characteristics I am convinced that my basic typology expresses something about youth ministry which is true not only in the UK but also in the US; we can group ourselves according to whether we work Outside-In or Inside-Out.

The reason for making this a key distinction throughout this book is my belief that it helps both youthworkers and church leaders to understand youth ministry better. One key advantage of this is that it brings a clarity at a theoretical level to the relationship between youth ministry (of whatever type) and the church. This does not just help in the strategic planning of the youth ministry, it is also fundamental in beginning to unravel the thorny issue of how the young people we work with might relate to the life of the local church.

My sense is that the question of young people and the church is increasingly seen, on both sides of the Atlantic, as the pivotal issue for youth ministry. For all the hype and financial investment in our activities, the key question is, "Are we helping young people to find Christ and grow in their faith?" At a theological level I am convinced that we can no longer with any credibility present youth ministry as a successful route to fulfil these two aims if we are not at the same time giving due consideration to how young people eventually find a place within the church. We can express this question in a variety of different ways: church could be seen as the body of

Christ, the community of believers, the local congregation, or the denomination. How we answer this question will depend on our particular theological commitments and organizational allegiances. While I do not want to get into these issues in any depth I am passionately committed to the view that we cannot avoid the question.

At the same time it seems clear that the church for its part must start to think much more imaginatively about the place of young people and youth ministry in relation to its ongoing life. This requires careful thought and creative solutions. The challenge therefore cuts both ways. In the final sections of this chapter I will try to set out the challenges and opportunities for youth ministry and the church as we seek a common way forward on this question of how to help young people find Christ and grow. I will also try to show how adopting the typology I set out might provide a way forward for dialogue. There are three key audiences for this discussion: parachurch youth ministries, the youth minister in the church, and church leaders.

The Bottom Line for Para-Church Youth Ministries ◆◆◆◆◆◆◆◆◆◆◆◆◆◆◆◆◆◆◆◆◆◆◆◆◆◆

Organizations such as Young Life or Youth For Christ need to think much more deeply about their relationship to the church. It seems to be increasingly the case that while these groups are still successful in reaching young people and proclaiming the gospel, there is a steady pattern developing in their work: young people may be turning to Christ, but they are often not finding their way into the local church. This trend is extremely alarming. In the past parachurch ministries could assume that young people would somehow connect up with a suitable church. This is less likely to be the case, however, because of the decline in church-going among the youth's parents and immediate family. Wider changes in contemporary culture also make long term allegiance to institutions much less acceptable.

All of this means that parachurch youth ministries need to start to consider how they can bridge the gap between church and the young people with whom they have significant contact. Bridging the gap may involve running experimental worship services for young people. For those working Outside-In there may be a need to develop expertise in how to plant new churches. For those working Inside-Out there may well be need to work with local congregations and church leaders on ways to develop specific youth congregations or services within existing churches. All of this inevitably means that some kind of understanding needs to be reached with local church leaders, church communities, and denominations. How this is done will depend on local church relationships and politics.

Parachurch organizations that take church seriously will have to start to do more than simply fundraise from individual church members. There is a need to bring church leaders together to discuss the problems of linking young people to worshipping congregations. Parachurch ministries will probably have to lead the way in educating churches on what the possible solutions might be. A key to this will be a basic understanding of what youth ministry—be it Outside-In or Inside-Out—is trying to achieve. It is increasingly the case in the UK that where youth ministry is successful para-church youth ministers have had to develop some kind of worship service or youth congregation. These ministers have realized that the churches are not equipped to do this job and are not in relationship with the young people in question. At the same time this has meant that delicate and imaginative negotiations have had to be undertaken to find the best way to connect the youth worship to the local church.

The Bottom Line for the Youth Minister in the Church ◆◆◆◆◆◆◆◆◆◆◆◆◆◆◆◆◆◆◆◆◆◆◆◆◆◆◆

The church-based youth minister has a commitment to an existing congregation and denominational organization. This makes his or her job much simpler. When it becomes clear that young people—either from an Inside-Out or an Outside-In ministry—are failing to hook up with the church, the youth minister must attempt to find the right way forward. It is at this point that the range of solutions comes into play.

At the one end of the spectrum it might be possible to develop some kind of worship event which runs parallel to the main activities of the local congregation. If this is successful it might be that some kind of regular weekly service could be put together. A key factor in all of this is that the youth minister needs to keep close to the rest of the staff team and in particular to the senior pastor. My own experience is that it can be helpful to involve other members of the staff in running this kind of event. Young people need to feel that they are free to do their own thing. It should however be possible to work with ministers and clergy to allow this to happen and at the same time express the basic connection between what the young people are doing and the leadership of the church. At the most basic level ministers may simply have to spend time with the young people on a regular basis.

If the youth minister is working Outside-In then at some point a new congregation may be the right way forward. If this is the case then it is essential that the youth minister works with the senior pastor and the denomination to follow the guidelines for this kind of initiative. For the sake of the young people it is essential that the youth minister ensures that everything happens in a way which is approved of by the local churches. Of course at times it is impossible to keep all parties happy, but every effort should be made to minimize conflict.

The Bottom Line for the Church Leader ◆◆◆◆◆◆◆

Church leaders are, most often, supportive of youth ministry. Sometimes, however, church leaders fail to understand exactly what is involved in youth ministry, breeding conflict between themselves and youth ministers.

How young people are to become a part of a regular worshipping congregation is the responsibility of the whole church. Church leaders need to address this question seriously. They need to get close to young people and the youth minister to first understand what are their needs and desires. It may well be that God is calling the young people to do something new and very different from what happens on a Sunday morning for the majority of people in a local church or indeed in the rest of the town or the city. The church leader needs to get a clear grasp of what is starting to emerge from the youth ministry in their neighborhood. Once they have done this their role is threefold.

First, they should take a leadership role in working with the young people and youth minister to develop a plan. They need to recognize that they may not have the vision or the practical skills to develop a new form of worship for young people. Their role is to hold together the creative team which might bring this about.

Second, they need to bless what happens. In most cases, new initiatives start very tentatively and with a good deal of disorganization. The church leader however needs to use his or her position to continually encourage and support what is happening. Young people need the blessing of their leaders in the faith. They need this in many cases above and beyond their need for guidance and advice. When church leaders trust in the Holy Spirit to guide young people church leaders can better resist the desire to control.

Blessing a new venture of this kind also involves a certain amount of advocacy. This could be with other ministers in the area, with parents of the young people, or with denominational structures. It is in many cases only the church leader who is able to play this role with any authority.

Third, the church leader needs to take responsibility for what happens. This may be difficult, especially when they are not running the new service or congregation directly. This is the role, however, of the church leader. There needs to be an agreed-upon system of accountability where young people and youth ministers report on a regular basis to the church leadership, since experiments do sometimes go wrong. The church leader needs to know when to intervene with what is happening in a service and when to allow things to continue on their own. In order to do this well they must know what is going on.

Questions to Ponder and Discuss

1. Are there youth ministers who get more out of youth camps and services than regular church? Are there ways in which some of us have escaped? Is it fair to say that those in parachurch organizations are not much concerned with how young people connect with the church?

2. This chapter states: "Youth ministry starts and ends with the church." Do you agree? How do young people need the church? What kind of a church do they need? How far can we go in accomodating church into the cultural styles of youth?

3. How do you define church? How flexible can we expect more traditional churches to be in accepting and working with youth churches? What do you and the young people you know want to say to your denomination, to your local church or parish? What kinds of alternative worship are needed? Do you agree that "youth ministry must take the church much more seriously"?

4. If young people outside church begin to form a faith community, do you agree that they need to be given the space to develop their own styles of worship and Christian expression? Would you encourage such youth churches to form and to develop, slowly in time, into intergenerational churches of their own?

5. What do you think about youth churches and youth worship services? How many youth churches do you know of? (There are many around the

world, especially in Europe.) What are some dangers of youth churches? What cautions or guidelines would you give them? What are the strengths of such churches?

6. This chapter presents the church as existing in three forms: missionary project, community group, and institution. Is this helpful?

7. This chapter's definition of missionary project includes all Christian youth organizations and church plants. Can it be evangelistic or social in emphasis? Do you think the church needs "prophetic witnesses" outside itself?

8. What have you received from this book? How will you use it? How will you pass it on?

Notes

CHAPTER 1: The Two Disciplines of Youth Ministry

1. By "traditions" I mean the historic practices of youthwork; "disciplines" are the methodologies that happen within those practices.

2. See the work of Frontier Youth Trust and in particular Terry Dunnell, *Mission and Young People at Risk* (London: Frontier Youth Trust, 1985).

3. Jon Langford, "Let's Get Spiritual," *Young People Now* (June 1994): 34, 35, and Martin Shaw "Religious Development," *Young People Now* (July 1994): 35.

4. Pete Ward, *Growing Up Evangelical* (London: SPCK, 1996).

5. For more on ideal types see David Jary and Julia Jary Collins, "Ideal Type," *Collins Dictionary of Sociology* (Glasgow: Harper-Collins, 1995).

6. I first saw this illustration in a training leaflet created by Mark Ashton, when he was head of Church Youth Fellowship Association.

7. Tricia Williams, *Christians in School* (Oxford: Scripture Union Press, 1985), 14.

8. Mark Ashton and Phil Moon, *Christian Youthwork* (Eastbourne: Monarch, 1995).

9. Ibid.

10. For a historical perspective on this see Ward, *Growing Up Evangelical,* 23ff.

11. Bob Mayo, *Gospel Exploded* (London: Triangle, 1996).

12. Ward, *Growing Up Evangelical,* 63ff.

13. Mark Smith, *Developing Youthwork* (Philadelphia: Open University, 1988), 1ff., and Kathleen Heaseman, *Evangelicals in Action* (London: Geoffrey Bles, 1962).

14. Roger Sainsbury, *From a Mersey Wall* (Oxford: Scripture Union Press, 1970), and Peter Stow, *Youth in the City* (London: Hodder & Stoughton, 1987).

15. Pip Wilson, *Gutter Feelings* (London: Hodder & Stoughton, 1985).

16. Ward, *Growing Up Evangelical*, 199ff.

17. Charles Kraft, *Christianity in Culture* (Maryknoll, N.Y.: Orbis, 1979), 5.

18. For more on this see Chapter 7.

19. I can't imagine that Clucas has ever written this down, but I am sure that he will be more than happy to explain his ideas at length if you care to contact him at Church Pastoral Aid Society, Tachbrook Park, Warwick, England.

20. I confess I have been guilty of this in the past.

CHAPTER 2: A Theology for Youth Ministry

1. See "A Theology for Youthwork," pages 23–38 in *Youth Apart* (London: Church House, 1996). I am indebted to Graham Cray, who played a large part in developing the theology sections of *Youth Apart*, for many of the insights in this chapter.

2. A rendering of John 20:27.

3. Mark 15:34.

4. Jurgen Moltmann, *The Crucified God* (London: SCM, 1974), 243.

5. Mark 8:34–35.

6. Dean Borgman, "Youth, Culture, and Media: Contemporary Youth Ministry," *Transformation* 11 (2, April/June 1994), 13.

7. Frances Young, *Sacrifice and the Death of Christ* (London: SCM, 1975).

8. F. W. Dillistone, "Redemption," pages 487–88 in Alan Richardson and John Bowden, eds., *A New Dictionary of Christian Theology* (London: SCM, 1983).

9. Ephesians 1:7.

10. Church of England. *The Alternative Service Book 1980*, (London: Clowes; SPCK: Cambridge University Press, 1980), an additional resource book to the Anglican Church's *Book of Common Prayer* (San Francisco: HarperSanFrancisco, 1991).

11. Isaac Watts, "When I Survey the Wondrous Cross." This hymn and others are used by Young in *Sacrifice and the Death of Christ*.

12. Karl Barth, *The Epistle to the Romans* (Oxford: Oxford University Press, 1933).

13. Ibid.

14. Alister McGrath, *Evangelicalism and the Future of Christianity* (London: Hodder & Stoughton, 1995), 137ff.

15. Mark 1:15.

16. Edward Schillebeeckx, *Jesus* (London: Fount, 1979) 206ff.; also Joachim Jeremias, *New Testament Theology* (Vol. 1; London: SCM, 1971), 118ff.

17. Used by kind permission of Anna Chakka George and Fiona Macleod.

18. This point was suggested to me by David Howell.

CHAPTER 3: The Incarnational Approach

1. Different employers have differing guidelines. The voluntary agencies have a duty to try to ensure that youthwork is "safe." Good advice and guidelines are generally available from denominational youth departments, such as the Anglican Diocesan Youth Officers.

2. Pete Ward, Sam Adams, and Jude Levermore, *Youthwork and How to Do It* (Oxford: Lynx, 1994), 21ff.; also Pete Ward, "Christian Relational Care," *Relational Youthwork* (ed. Pete Ward; Oxford: Lynx, 1995).

3. This is a phrase I first heard from Arnie Jacobs of Young Life who inspired me and a number of others to try to do youthwork better.

4. For more on this contact Steve Connor at Christians in Sport, P.O. Box 93, Oxford, Great Britain.

5. Jude Levermore, "Interpersonal Skills for Youth Workers," pages 25–44 in *Youthwork and How to Do It*.

6. Ibid.

7. For more on Jim Rayburn III, see *Dance Children Dance* (Carol Stream, Ill.: Tyndale, 1984); also Mark Senter, *The Coming Revolution in Youth Ministry* (Wheaton: Victor, 1992), 17ff.

8. Pete Ward, *Youth Culture and the Gospel* (Glasgow: HarperCollins, 1992), and Pete Ward, *Worship and Youth Culture* (Glasgow: HarperCollins, 1993).

9. Mayo, *Gospel Exploded.*

10. These matters are dealt with at length in Chapters 5 and 6.

11. Phil Moon, *Hanging in There* (Eastbourne: Monarch, 1994), 58.

12. For an alternative approach to this which combines contact work with a nucleus group, see Mark Senter, "Emerging Patterns of Youth Ministry at the End of the Century," pages 105–31 in *Relational Youthwork.*

CHAPTER 4: Popular Culture

1. Much of what follows in this chapter is based on Jim McGuigan, *Cultural Populism* (London: Routledge, 1992), and Mike Brake, *Comparative Youth Culture* (London: Routledge & Kegan Paul, 1985).

2. Ibid., 2.

3. Louis J. Luzbetak, *The Church and Cultures* (Maryknoll, N.Y.: Orbis, 1988), 12ff.

4. Richard Hoggart, *The Uses of Literacy* (London: Chatto and Windus, 1957); E. P. Thompson, *The Making of the English Working Class* (London: Victor Gollancz, 1963); Raymond Williams, *Culture and Society* (London: Chatto and Windus, 1958).

5. Ioan Davies, *Cultural Studies and Beyond* (London: Routledge, 1995), 35ff.

6. Brake, *Comparative Youth Culture*, 3.

7. Stuart Hall and Tony Jefferson, *Resistance through Rituals* (London: Hutchinson, 1975), 5ff.

8. See *Resistance through Rituals*.

9. Peter Marsh, Elizabeth Rosser, and Rom Harre, *The Rules of Disorder* (London: Routledge & Kegan Paul, 1978).

10. Quentin Schultze, Roy Anker, James Bratt, William Romanowski, John Worst, and Lambert Zuidervaart, *Dancing in the Dark* (Grand Rapids: Eerdmans, 1991).

11. Neil Postman, *Amusing Ourselves to Death* (New York: Penguin, 1985).

12. John Buckeridge editorial in *Youthwork* (August/September 1992): 2.

13. For more on this see Ward, *Growing Up Evangelical*.

14. Paul Willis, *Common Culture* (Milton Keynes: Open University, 1990), 1ff.

15. Ibid., 9ff.

16. John Fiske, *Understanding Popular Culture* (London: Routledge, 1989), 28ff.

17. Ibid., 24.

18. Willis, *Common Culture*, 13.

19. Ibid., 13.

20. Ibid., 141–45.

21. McGuigan, *Cultural Populism*.

22. Andrew Walker, *Telling the Story* (London: SPCK, 1996).

23. As further reading for this chapter, see Andrew Calcutt, *Arrested Development: Pop Culture and the Erosion of Adulthood* (Washington, D.C.: Cassell, 1998); Jonathon S. Epstein (ed.), *Youth Culture: Identity in a Postmodern World* (Malden, Mass.: Blackwell, 1998); Patricia Hersch, *A Tribe Apart: A Journey into the Heart of American Adolescence* (New York: Fawcett Columbine, 1998); and Tracey Skelton and Gill Valentine (eds.), *Cool Places: Geographies of Youth Cultures* (New York: Routledge, 1998).

CHAPTER 5: Youthwork and the Incarnation of the Word

1. Ward, *Youth Culture and the Gospel*.

2. For more on dynamic equivalents translation see Kraft, *Christianity in Culture*.

3. Karl Barth, "The Strange New World Within the Bible," pages 28–51 in *The Word of God and the Word of Man* (London: Hodder & Stoughton, 1928).

4. Eugene Peterson, *The Message* (Colorado Springs: NavPress, 1994); Walter Wangerin, *The Book of God* (Oxford: Lion, 1996).

5. Dietrich Bonhoeffer, *The Cost of Discipleship* (London: SCM, 1948).

CHAPTER 6: Getting Started: Two Case Studies

1. For more on this, see Young, *Sacrifice and the Death of Christ.*

2. Walker, *Telling the Story*, 12ff.

3. Luke 4:18.

4. Luke 5:30–32 RSV.

5. Jeremias, *New Testament Theology,* 118.

6. Schillebeeckx, *Jesus' Fount*, 206.

7. Matthew 22:1–10.

8. Luke 7:36–50.

9. Luke 7:44–46.

10. Matthew 25:14–30.

11. Luke 12:19–21.

12. Mark 1:14–20.

13. Tony Campolo, *The Church and the American Teenager* (Grand Rapids: Zondervan, 1989), 32ff.

14. Based on a personal conversation with Tony Campolo.

15. I am indebted to the work of successive groups of Oxford Youth Works students for these two case studies. As presented these are composite pictures based on and modified from a number of student presentations.